Thomas Jefferson's

Monticello

(Pages ii–iii) Monticello's southwest front. In 1787 Jefferson wrote to George Gilmer, "I am as happy no where else and in no other society, and all my wishes end, where I hope my days will end, at Monticello. Too many scenes of happiness mingle themselves with all the recollections of my native woods and fields, to suffer them to be supplanted in my affection by any other."

(Pages iv–v) Vineyards in winter. Because of documentary evidence that grapevines at Monticello were "espaliered," a permanent structure based on an eighteenth-century American grape trellis was constructed. Today, the vineyards feature several Jefferson-related European varieties grafted on hardy, pest-resistant native rootstock.

(Pages vi–vii) Jefferson's Greenhouse, or South Piazza. Margaret Bayard Smith said of the just-completed room in 1809: "The arched piazza beyond, was ultimately sashed in glass, and converted into a flower conservatory, so that the windows and glass doors of the library opened upon both its beauty and its fragrance."

Library of Congress Cataloging-in-Publication Data

Thomas Jefferson's Monticello
      p. cm.
    Includes bibliographical references (p.) and index.
    ISBN 1-882886-18-6 (alk. paper)
    1. Monticello (Va.)—Pictorial works. 2. Jefferson, Thomas, 1743-1826—Homes and haunts—Virginia—Albemarle County—Pictorial works. 3. Monticello (Va.)—History. I. Thomas Jefferson Foundation.

E332.74.T48 2002
975.5'482—dc21

          2002016138

This book was made possible by support from the
Martin S. and Luella Davis Publications Endowment.

Edited and coordinated by Beth L. Cheuk
Designed by Gibson Design Associates
Printed in the United Kingdom by Butler & Tanner
Distributed by
    The University of North Carolina Press
    Chapel Hill, North Carolina 27515-2288
    1-800-848-6224

Contents

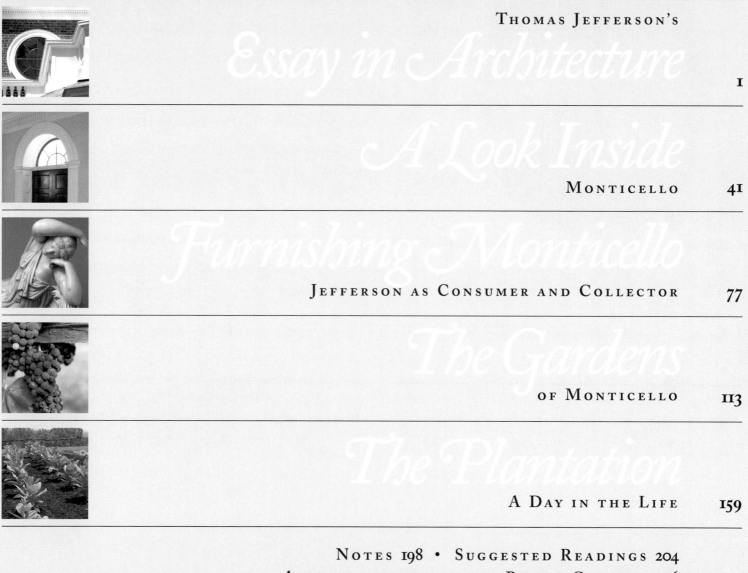

Foreword

As Wendell Garrett so eloquently notes in his preface to this book, Thomas Jefferson is a figure marked by paradox. Given the autobiographical nature of Monticello, it is appropriate that Jefferson's "essay in architecture" embodies the same theme. Built on the American frontier, Monticello reflects the design sensibilities of the ancient world. A symbol of liberty, it was constructed with slave labor and surrounded by plantation sites where enslaved men and women lived and labored. Celebrated for its beauty, the house was criticized in Jefferson's time for its incongruence. Architecture aside, Monticello's visitors observed its "strange" and "odd" assemblage of European art, Native American artifacts, natural specimens, and mechanical marvels. Even Jefferson's lovely gardens advanced a dual and seemingly contradictory goal of being both ornamental and scientific. In short, Monticello, like its celebrated owner, is complex and fascinating, and we have long awaited a full-length, richly illustrated treatment of this treasure, the only American house on the United Nations' list of World Heritage Sites.

To set the stage for this book, we are delighted to have a preface written by Wendell Garrett, an expert in Americana and longtime Trustee of the Thomas Jefferson Foundation, the private, nonprofit organization that owns and operates

Monticello. Our own scholarly staff contributed the essays, and a host of photographers, including Robert Lautman and Edward Owen, shared their talents. Gibson Design Associates gathered all these elements and brought the book to life, and Beth Cheuk coordinated the project from start to finish.

We are grateful not only to the talented individuals who have made contributions to this volume, but also to the many individuals who, through their generosity, support the Foundation's efforts to preserve and share Monticello, its landscape, and its collection. We are equally appreciative of those who give or lend precious artifacts for display at Monticello. The richness of Monticello lies in its authenticity. Amazingly, the house appears today largely as Jefferson knew it, down to original brick and much of the original glass; the gardens were restored to match the remaining depressions on the West Lawn; archaeological artifacts illuminate our understanding of slavery at Monticello; and the contents of the house are strikingly original, whether Jefferson's art, his dinnerware, or his boots. It is our hope that this book captures Monticello's authenticity, as well as its readers' imagination. Of course, no book can adequately convey all that is Monticello, but we hope that this one entrances you and makes you wish to see Jefferson's "little mountain" for yourself.

— Daniel P. Jordan
President, Thomas Jefferson Foundation

Preface

THOMAS JEFFERSON IS THE ONE AMERICAN STATESMAN WHO IS TIMELESS: not only is he the central, most familiar figure in American history, but he also is, of all the Founding Fathers, indeed of all the men of the eighteenth century, the most contemporary. His brilliant formulation and championship of the fundamental doctrines of human freedom and individual liberty are as relevant now as they were in his lifetime. He proclaimed that freedom "is the most sacred cause that ever man was engaged in." Without the "precious blessing" of liberty, he said, life has no sense and no dignity. Lincoln better than anyone else comprehended the basic ideas of democracy's most outspoken champion when he wrote, "The principles of Jefferson are the definitions and axioms of free society."

No leader in the period of the American Enlightenment was as articulate, as wise, as conscious of the implications and consequences of a free society as was he. Both in his public and his private life he addressed himself continually to problems of permanent and universal interest. What he wrote and what he did—about the nature of society and of government, the relations of man to government, the meaning of republicanism and democracy, the significance of education and of toleration and of experimentation to democracy—are as relevant today as during the eighteenth century. To the end of his life his opinions on many subjects varied as his experience ripened—but he never wavered in his faith in government of the people by and for themselves, holding that "The people are the only sure reliance for the preservation of our liberty." He held that all men are created equal, that they possess certain inalienable rights, and that governments derive their just powers from the consent of the governed. That unwavering trust in the dependability, wisdom, and honesty of the common literate individual is his greatest legacy. Woodrow Wilson

Thomas Jefferson's
Essay in Architecture

In March of 1809 Thomas Jefferson was at long last liberated from what he called the "splendid misery"[1] of the presidency of the United States, free to begin the evening of his life in retirement at Monticello. The event coincided with the essential completion of a house he had begun more than forty years earlier and transformed, beginning in 1796, from an eight-room to a twenty-one-room dwelling. The finish joinery, plastering, and painting alone took more than ten years of steady work to complete. What Jefferson created—for he was indeed its architect—was unlike any other house in the United States, and not just because it was the first house in this country to have a dome. It was unusual in both plan and elevation. Jefferson himself acknowledged that it ranked "among the curiosities of the neighborhood,"[2] and apart from its setting, which few could fault, apparently many who saw the house found it too idiosyncratic to be pleasing or even comprehensible. One visitor, some thirteen years after Jefferson's death, called it "a monument of ingenious extravagance ... without unity or uniformity, upon which architecture seem[s] to have exerted, if not exhausted, the versatility of her genius." The critic went on to state: "We will venture to say that Mr. Jefferson had no distinct conception of any design when he commenced building, but enlarged, added and modi-

---

by William L. Beiswanger, Robert H. Smith Director of Restoration at Monticello fied as his ingenuity contrived, until this incomprehensible pile reached this acme of its destiny in which it stands at present, still indeed unfinished."[3] It is true that Monticello lacks the purity and geometric simplicity of Jefferson's other buildings, such as the Rotunda at the University of Virginia or Poplar Forest, his octagonal retreat in Bedford County, Virginia. By contrast, Monticello showed all the signs of a modified and evolving plan, which is perhaps why he called it his "essay in architecture."[4]

He began the essay in 1768 at the age of twenty-five, the year he contracted with a Mr. Moore to level an area 250 feet square at the northeast end of the mountaintop.[5] It is clear from Jefferson's surviving drawings and notes that even in this early period he served as his own architect. In this art he was self-taught, gaining knowledge and inspiration from books and close observation. Monticello was, as far as

Jefferson's freehand drawing of Monticello shows the north and south bows that were added to the house c. 1777. The sketch could date from his years in Paris (1784–89), when he began thinking about enlarging the house. On the verso is a plan for adding two first-floor rooms.

we know, the first of his many architectural projects and, as it turns out, the most richly documented. Of the more than seven hundred architectural drawings and notes in Jefferson's hand, nearly half relate to the house and plantation at Monticello.[6]

For the most part, Jefferson rejected the architectural tradition established in Virginia. Compared even to dwellings elsewhere in the American colonies at that time, his drawing of the elevation of the house reveals a stricter—almost academic—application of classical sources and the Roman architectural orders. In one sense the façade of the first Monticello was a mathematical exercise in the use of the classical orders, and in this regard the young architect was guided principally by Andrea Palladio and his *Four*

The marquis de Chastellux, who visited Monticello in 1782, said that the house "resembled none of the others seen in this country," and that Thomas Jefferson was "the first American who has consulted the Fine Arts to know how he should shelter himself from the weather."

Jefferson's drawing of the house from the early 1770s reflects his rejection of the architectural tradition in Virginia and his interest in a stricter application of classical form as he understood it from the published works of the sixteenth-century architect and theorist Andrea Palladio.

Books of Architecture, first published in 1570.[7] When the marquis de Chastellux saw the house under construction in 1782, he went so far as to announce its uniqueness to the world, stating unequivocally that it "resembled none of the others seen in this country."[8]

Jefferson began by first constructing a rather modest six-room house. On the first floor was a parlor flanked by a chamber and a dining room, and on the second level, two bedrooms and a lofty study to house his growing library. It was about 1776 that Jefferson's propensity for alteration first surfaced in a significant way. He modified the already existing southwest (garden) front by adding a two-story canted bay projection to the parlor and study, and added one-story rooms, also of a partial octagonal shape, to the dining room and chamber. During the period of the 1770s he also devised a scheme for linking an impressive array of support rooms (dependencies) to the cellars of the house by L-shaped wings concealed in the hillside. This scheme, however, was not constructed until after 1800, and then only in a modified and greatly curtailed form. But it was this eight-room house and the plans for its completion, including ideas for decorating some of the rooms "entirely in the antique style," that impressed the marquis de Chastellux, and prompted the remarkable comment that Jefferson was "the first American who has consulted the Fine Arts to know how he should shelter himself from the weather."[9]

The South Pavilion, completed in the fall of 1770, was the first brick building at Monticello. Below the chamber was a kitchen, later moved to the angle of the Southeast Terrace. The pavilion was remodeled in 1808 at which time the doorway leading to the terrace was added.

(Below) Although the scheme for the L-shaped terraces that link the pavilions to the house dates from the 1770s, it was not executed until after 1800, and then only in modified form. This terrace landscape is perhaps the most universally satisfying aspect of Jefferson's design for Monticello.

The shell of the house was basically completed—certainly habitable—by 1784, when Jefferson departed for France on what would become a five-year diplomatic mission. The evidence suggests, however, that he had not completed—perhaps not even begun—the interior finish work such as the moldings and plastering. This might explain his comment to George Wythe in 1794 that he was "living in a brick-kiln … my house, in it's *[sic]* present state, is nothing better."[10]

While living in Paris, he experienced firsthand a new level of refinement in domestic architecture. The elegant townhouse that he rented on the corner of the Champs-Elysées and the rue de Berri had modern conveniences such as flush toilets and skylights that transformed spaces with diffused light.[11] There were the requisite formal "rooms of entertainment" and also a variety of private and intimate spaces that greatly enhanced comfort and convenience. The grouping of these spaces to form what could be called apartments was particularly an cyc-opener for Jefferson. By contrast, the plan of the house he left behind in Virginia must have seemed formal and stiff.

In 1796, acting on a new plan, Jefferson began a dramatic transformation of Monticello. The upper story was removed, the northeast front extended, and a new second level created for bedrooms within the height of the first floor. He referred to the new upper rooms as the "Mezzaninos."[12]

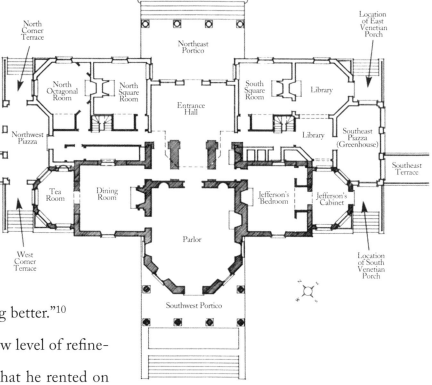

Plan of the first floor of Monticello as remodeled, beginning in 1796, and completed by 1809. The superimposed plan of the earlier house is indicated by the hatched walls.

In 1796, acting on a new plan, Jefferson began a dramatic transformation of Monticello. The upper story was removed, the northeast front (shown above) extended, and a new second level created within the height of the original first floor. The appearance suggests a one-story house.

(Opposite) The dome, constructed in 1800, was the first on a house in America. Jefferson based the proportions on the ancient Temple of Vesta in Rome. Although the portico and the dome are the central feature of the southwest (garden) front, the unifying elements are the entablature and balustrade carried around the perimeter of the building.

*The Northeast Portico frames a
recessed arcaded wall. The piers
between the doors and windows
are actually wood over brick, sand–
painted in imitation of finely tooled
sandstone. The stone columns date
from the early house and were reused
when the house was enlarged in 1796.*

The square windows for this mezzanine level are compressed between the main entablature and the cornice of the window below. Inside, the sills are only seven inches above the floor. On the third floor, three additional bedrooms are concealed in the northeast attic and lighted by skylights. The overall exterior appearance suggests a one-story house—an idea consistent with the progressive French thinking on domestic architecture so much admired by Jefferson.

For the west front he lowered the height of the second-floor study by eight feet and over it constructed a dome inspired by the Temple of Vesta at Rome illustrated in Giacomo Leoni's handsome edition of Palladio's *Four Books of Architecture*. By necessity, Jefferson had to adapt the circular form to an octagonal plan, but the proportions of the dome (one-third of a circle) and the rise and projection of the three steps at its base were preserved.[13]

Glass doors and triple-sash windows, which also serve as doorways, connect the spacious Entrance Hall to the Northeast Portico. The linkage of these two spaces is further suggested by the floor and glossy floorcloth, both painted grass green at the suggestion of the portrait painter Gilbert Stuart.

The Doric portico and dome are the central focus of the façade, but the unifying horizontal elements of this neoclassical essay are the Doric entablature and balustrade carried around the perimeter of the building. Jefferson's use, however, of a Chinese lattice railing on top of the house seems to challenge the hierarchy if not the primacy of the classical orders.

Jefferson's plan called for retaining the rooms on the main floor that ranged along the southwest front and for advancing the northeast front to accommodate a large entrance hall/museum, a library, and three bedrooms. The old and new spaces in the wings were to be organized around lateral passageways off the Entrance Hall. He rejected the idea of a great staircase in the Entrance Hall and instead provided a much smaller one in each of the passageways. He reasoned that "great staircases … are expensive & occupy a space which would make a good room in every story."[14] But it was also consistent with his view that the merely ceremonial should be avoided. Jefferson's apartment occupied most of the south end of the house while two guest bedrooms were on the north side. The chamber on the south side was used as a family sitting room and schoolroom, although it has an alcove for a bed, as do the two guest chambers. Jefferson summarized his approach for reorganizing the house in a letter to John Brown in 1797: "In Paris particularly all the new & good houses are of a single story, that is of the height of 16. or 18. f. generally, & the whole of it given to the rooms of entertainment; but in the parts where there are bedrooms they have two tiers of them of from 8. to 10. f. high each, with a small private staircase."[15] In following the logic of the French *parti*, Jefferson created an asymmetrical distribution of high-ceilinged rooms for the main floor. The result was the irregular plan of the second level. Four chambers, each with bed alcoves, ranged along the northeast front. Over the Cabinet was the room Jefferson called the "Appendix," and next to it a nursery (for grandchildren) tucked into the low-ceilinged room above the Greenhouse.[16] The cantilevered gallery in the Entrance Hall connected the north and south spaces.

Jefferson's asymmetrical distribution of high-ceilinged rooms for the main floor resulted in the irregular plan of the second level. This asymmetry is not evident, however, when one views the southwest (garden) front.

It is remarkable that Jefferson, a widower since 1782, would see a need to more than double the size of his house. When he began the enterprise he wrote a friend, "I am uncovering & repairing my house, which during my absence had gone much to decay." However, he went on to explain, "I make some alterations in it with a greater eye to convenience than I had when younger."[17] Convenience, one could argue, was largely self-centered. Even so, when his family joined him in 1809, the house apparently functioned well.

In that first year of his retirement there were living at Monticello his eldest daughter Martha, her husband Thomas Mann Randolph, and six of the eight Randolph children, ages ranging from eight months to twelve years. In time three additional children would be born, and Jefferson's sister Anna Scott Marks would join this domestic scene. His apartment, for indeed it could be called that, occupied the width of the southeast side of the house and about one-third the length of the long southwest (garden) front. At its core were the Bedroom, Cabinet (study), and Book Room. Although the first two rooms existed in modified form in the pre-1796 house, the Book Room was an addition. Its incorporation into the apartment marked a significant change from the earlier version of Monticello, where the library above the parlor was probably the second most impressive architectural space in the house. Its elimination when Jefferson decided to spread out all his principal rooms on the ground floor shows how far he had come to value convenience over ceremony and architectural display.

Jefferson's suite is L-shaped and the spaces are connected in such a way that one hesitates to call them three separate rooms. Besides conventional doorways, features such as a bed in an alcove open on both sides, and arches—one broad and elliptical and the other narrow and semicircular—are employed as transitions from one space to another. Variety is introduced by changes in ceiling heights and in the amount and quality of natural light admitted. The Bedroom, for example, is nearly nineteen feet high and flooded with light from a large skylight and a triple-sash window. To moderate the light and heat in summer, Jefferson designed a louvered blind with movable slats to close over the skylight.

A bed alcove was first planned where the elliptical arch is now. But Jefferson changed his mind and decided to extend his Cabinet and Book Room the full width of the building. Margaret Bayard Smith found the "numerous divisions and arches" in Jefferson's apartment disappointing, and thought that one large room would have been more impressive.

The climax of the Jefferson's apartment is the Chamber. This nearly nineteen-foot-high space is lighted by a skylight and a triple-sash window. Above the bed alcove is a closet vented and illuminated by three elliptical openings and reached by a steep stair or ladder in the closet to the right of the alcove.

Jefferson chose for his own chamber the Ionic entablature from the Roman temple commonly known as Fortuna Virilis (Manly Fortune). The source was Jombert's edition of the Parallel de l'Architecture Antique avec la Moderne. *The frieze, however, was based on Desgodetz's* Édifices Antiques de Rome, *which depicts with greater accuracy and detail the combination of bucrania, putti, candelabra, and swags.*

The bed alcove, which dates from the remodeling of the house in 1796, replaced a narrow doorway that separated the Chamber from the Cabinet. Beyond the alcove is the fireplace with the frieze repeating the form chosen for the room entablature. Jefferson provided his joiners with a full-size drawing of the fireplace moldings (shown in background).

Glass doors lead from the Book Room to the Southeast Piazza, another space in Jefferson's apartment.

(Opposite) In writing to William Hamilton on March 1, 1808, Jefferson observed, "My green house is only a piazza adjoining my study, because I mean it for nothing more than some oranges, Mimosa Farnesiana & a very few things of that kind." The piazza was also to house an aviary for Jefferson's pet mockingbirds.

In his scheme, he stated, "my blinds open back on hinges as in the winter we want both the light and warmth of the sun."[18] The two other spaces in Jefferson's suite (above which are the family bedrooms on the second floor) are ten feet high and lighted by more conventional windows and glass doors.

The irregular layout of the apartment was noteworthy for its time in a country where symmetry and balance were so highly esteemed. Margaret Bayard Smith, who was otherwise an ardent admirer of Jefferson, sided with the critics, confessing, "I own I was much disappointed in its appearance, and I do not think with its numerous divisions and arches it is as impressive as one large room would have been."[19]

Mrs. Smith referred to the apartment as Jefferson's "sanctum sanctorum."[20] There he spent the morning hours until breakfast, after which he visited his gardens or rode off to inspect his plantation. His granddaughter Ellen Wayles Randolph Coolidge remembered:

As the day, in summer, grew warmer he retired to his own apartments .... Here he remained until about one o'clock, occupied in reading, writing, looking over papers, etc.

My mother would sometimes send me with a message to him. A gentle knock, a call of "come in." and I would enter, with a mixed feeling of love and reverence, and some pride in being the bearer of a communication ....[21]

Perhaps the most remarkable feature of the apartment was the integration of three outdoor rooms that added greatly to Jefferson's comfort, convenience, and pleasure. Each is basically a porch and each is directly connected to the apartment by folding glass doors. In square footage the three spaces equal nearly half the area of the Bedroom, Cabinet, and Book Room. Isaac Weld, who was at Monticello the year before

the remodeling of 1796 was underway, alluded to at least one of the outdoor spaces when he observed: "A large apartment is laid out for a library and museum, meant to extend the entire breadth of the house, the windows of which are to open into an extensive green house and aviary."[22] The museum was ultimately established in the Entrance Hall; the greenhouse and aviary were planned for the arcaded loggia that Jefferson called the Southeast Piazza, which projects from the center of the southeast façade. This neatly plastered room is nearly twelve feet high and has window sashes on three sides that can be raised to doorway height. Above it on the second floor is a child's nursery.

(Following pages) Longitudinal section through the southwest-front rooms rendered in watercolor by Floyd E. Johnson in 1986. The narrow space above Jefferson's alcove bed was for out-of-season clothes. The second-floor room above Jefferson's Cabinet was granddaughter Ellen's bedroom. The Venetian Porch, adjoining the Cabinet and recreated in 2000, is not shown.

Windows that double as doorways appear throughout the first floor of Monticello, including this one leading from the Greenhouse to the Southeast Terrace. In this version, the two lower sashes can be raised to the height of a door.

Although there was sufficient light and ventilation, the piazza was apparently not heated, and its success as a greenhouse was limited. However, with the addition of a workbench it functioned admirably as a shop, in which, we are told, Jefferson made models and other small things of wood and metal.[23]

Weld's comment could be interpreted to mean that the aviary was to be a separate room, yet an entry by Jefferson in his building notebook indicates that the piazza was the intended location: "S.E. Piazza. from impost to top of architrave an Aviary to occupy breadth of recess only."[24] From his note it appears that the floor of the cage was to be aligned with the base of the arched portion of the windows (the imposts)—hence high enough to walk under. The top of the cage was to be level with the top of the window architrave, which in this case is at ceiling height. "Breadth of recess only" is a little more puzzling but very likely it refers to the back area of the piazza between the side arches and the Library. Although nothing remains of an aviary at Monticello, it is almost certain that somewhere within his apartment he housed his pet mockingbirds. He had three of them in Washington. Mrs. Smith described one:

In the window recesses were stands for the flowers and plants which it was his delight to attend and among his roses and geraniums was suspended the cage of his favorite mocking-bird, which he cherished with peculiar fondness, not only for its melodious powers, but for its uncommon intelligence and affectionate disposition, of which qualities he gave surprising instances. It was the constant companion of his solitary and studious hours. Whenever he was alone he opened

Glass doors connect the Cabinet to the South Venetian Porch. Granddaughter Ellen recalled, "His summer study, where he remained all the morning hours of the fine season, was under a room which was for a long time my own chamber, and, the windows being open, I heard him frequently thus singing the old Psalm tunes, or the Scotch melodies in which in spite of his love for Italian music, he always took great pleasure." Whether the reference is to the Venetian porch or the Cabinet is uncertain.

the cage and let the bird fly about the room. After flitting for a while from one object to another, it would alight on his table and regale him with its sweetest notes, or perch on his shoulder and take its food from his lips. Often when he retired to his chamber it would hop up the stairs after him and while he took his siesta, would sit on his couch and pour forth its melodious strains.[25]

Interior of the South Venetian Porch. The light inside the "porticle" can be modulated by adjusting the angle of the slats in the door blinds or by folding back the double-tier doors in a variety of combinations. One can even remove the lunettes within the arches.

The birds were shipped to Monticello when Jefferson left Washington in 1809, and on April 25 he was able to send the reassuring word, "My birds arrived here in safety and are the delight of every hour."[26]

Flanking the Southeast Piazza are small enclosed terraces that could be entered from the piazza or the adjoining Cabinet or Library, whence one could descend to the lawn. Jefferson sometimes called them "Porticles," a word that suggests small porches or porticos.[27] And he also called them his Venetian Porches—a clear reference to the jalousies (louvered blinds) that constitute the walls.[28] Although they were removed about 1893, they were recorded in early artists' views and photographs, and recreated in 2000 based on those views and Jefferson's plan for the South Venetian Porch.[29] This plan, which details his scheme for door blinds, probably dates from 1805, when he was ordering similar exterior louvered shutters for the Southeast Piazza.[30] Within each doorway there were to be two tiers of double bi-fold blinds with movable slats, each tier four feet high. These were to be the same thickness as the walls: three and one-half inches. The blinds were to be hinged so that when not in use they could swing clear of the arches and fold compactly against the piers. Nowhere does Jefferson mention the function of the Venetian Porches. Privacy might have been a consideration, but more likely they were valued as cool retreats from the sun—a view consistent with his claim that "under the beaming, constant and almost vertical sun of Virginia, shade is our Elysium."[31] It is easy to imagine the pleasure of step-

(Opposite) The Venetian Porches flanking the Southeast Piazza (Greenhouse) served as cool retreats from the sun. Jefferson could justify them by his belief that the design of the house should be "subordinated to the law of convenience." That he struggled to balance convenience and aesthetics is evident in his response to his joiner's query whether there should be a railing on each roof. Jefferson responded, "I do not propose any Chinese railing on the two Porticles at the doors of my Cabinet, because it would make them more conspicuous to the prejudice of the Piazza & it's [sic] pediment as the principal object. The intention was that they should be as obscure as possible that they might not disturb the effect of their principal."

The scheme for uniting the house and dependencies in L-shaped wings is not unlike examples of villas designed by Andrea Palladio and known to Jefferson from books. The distinction, however, is that the dwelling in a Palladian villa is typically at the head of a courtyard enclosed by the service buildings. But at Monticello Jefferson took advantage of the sloping site and constructed the dependencies in the hillside, thereby providing access to the service rooms at ground level while preserving uninterrupted views of the landscape from the windows of the house. In short, what he created—unique in American architecture—was a Palladian scheme turned inside out.

ping from the Library or Cabinet into either of these enclosures—perhaps the east one in the morning and the south in the afternoon. The South Venetian Porch might have been, in fact, Jefferson's Summer Study. Ellen, whose room was above his Cabinet, remembers overhearing her grandfather in his apartment:

His voice continued wonderfully sweet and unbroken even to the last years of his life. He had the habit of singing low or what is called humming in the intervals between his various employments, when he rose from his writing table or reading chair and walked about his rooms. His summer study, where he remained all the morning hours of the fine season, was under a room which was for a long time my

own chamber, and, the windows being open, I heard him frequently thus singing the old Psalm tunes, or the Scotch melodies in which in spite of his love for Italian music, he always took great pleasure.[32]

View of the Southeast Terrace from the piazza. This terrace was an extension of Jefferson's private apartment.

Regardless of whether the South Venetian Porch or the Cabinet was the Summer Study, Ellen's account reveals her grandfather's habit of seasonal changes within his quarters.

The final component of Jefferson's extended apartment is the raised terrace that leads from the Southeast Piazza to a two-story outchamber known as the South Pavilion. A similar terrace arrangement is found on the northwest side of the house. Both terraces are L-shaped, and beneath the nine-foot-wide deck that leads from the piazzas to the angles are passages that link the cellar of the house to dependencies located under the much broader section of terraces. The scheme is not unlike that of some Palladian villas, where the dwelling is flanked by service buildings forming a U-shaped courtyard. However, at Monticello, Jefferson minimized the sense of courtyard and opened views of the landscape from the house by concealing the dependencies in the hillside. In short, what he created was a Palladian scheme turned inside out. Although these terraces were not constructed until the first decade of the nineteenth century, the initial idea dates from the 1770s and recalls a suggestion made by Lord Kames in his essay "Gardening and Architecture" in the *Elements of Criticism*, a work known to Jefferson by 1771. Kames had proposed an artificial walk elevated high above the plain—an airy walk that would extend and vary the prospect and elevate the mind.[33] From Jefferson's elevated walkway there are views of the gardens and impressive vistas of the plain to the south and east. The design was unique for its time not only in this country but also perhaps in Great Britain and Europe, where terraces connected to buildings were usually raised on much higher platforms. Jefferson's walkways are only about four feet above grade and are more intimately connected to the landscape. The sense is that the main floor of the house extends into the garden. This is perhaps the most universally satisfying aspect of the design of Monticello, and one has only to step from the house onto the wooden terrace and hear the sound of footsteps to

experience it. Yet for all its humanism, the image that comes to mind is also patrician, for beneath the walkways, buried in the hillside and therefore out of sight, are the activities of those who labored in his service.

Although Jefferson's apartment best demonstrates the breadth of his thinking about extended living spaces, there are similarly conceived areas on all sides of the house. Projecting from the northwest end of the building is another piazza that outwardly resembles the Greenhouse in its arched openings, exterior entablature, and pediment. However, it is not enclosed with sashes nor is it plastered; it is a true open loggia. The ceiling is also much higher, owing to the absence of a second-floor

The Northwest Terrace. Granddaughter Ellen recalled, "From this northern terrace the view is sublime; and here Jefferson and his company were accustomed to sit, bare-headed, in the summer until bed-time, having neither dew nor insects to annoy them. Here, perhaps, has been assembled more love of liberty, virtue, wisdom, and learning than on any other private spot in America."

room. Embellishing the otherwise stark interior is a Doric entablature based on one from the ancient Roman Baths of Diocletian, where the face of the sun god is repeated in the metopes.

Flanking the piazza are two small terraces with stairs leading to the lawn. Although basically similar to their southeast counterparts, they were never enclosed. The four corner terraces are probably what Jefferson called the "Angular Portals," for each provides a secondary entry to the house through raised triple-sash windows or

French doors. Another feature of each corner terrace is a built-in planting bed that fills the triangular void between the stairs and the canted wall of the house. We are told that violets grew within the triangle outside Jefferson's Cabinet window.[34]

The raised walkway that leads from the Northwest Piazza to the pavilion was known as the "public terrace," which implies that the southeast one was reserved for the family or perhaps for Jefferson alone.[35] Edmund Bacon, a longtime overseer, recalled, "Mr. Jefferson was always an early riser—arose at daybreak or before. The sun never found him in bed. I used sometimes to think, when I went up there *very* early in the morning, that I would find him in bed; but there he would be before me, walking on the terrace."[36] Later in the day, according to Ellen, Jefferson would reemerge from his rooms "before sunset to walk on the terrace or the lawn, to see his grandchildren run races, or to converse with his family and friends."[37] So important was this ritual to the aging man that when the snow fell, according to Ellen's sister Virginia, "we would go out, as soon as it stopped, to clear it off the terraces with shovels, that he might have his usual walk on them without treading in snow."[38]

No doubt it was the Northwest Terrace that many had in mind when they mentioned "a favorite promenade in the evening and in damp weather."[39] From here there are views of the village of Charlottesville, the valley, and the Blue Ridge Mountains beyond. Ellen remembered it well: "From this northern terrace the view is sublime; and here Jefferson and his company were accustomed to sit, bare-headed, in the summer until bed-time, having neither dew nor insects to annoy them. Here, perhaps, has been assembled more love of liberty, virtue, wisdom, and learning than on any other private spot in America."[40]

Glimpse of the Northwest Piazza from the second-floor north passage window. Outwardly, the piazza resembles the Greenhouse in its arched openings, exterior entablature, and pediment. Within it is a very different space: it is a true open loggia with a much higher ceiling owing to the absence of a second-floor room. The only embellishment to this stark brick interior is the massive Doric entablature based on an example from the ancient Roman Baths of Diocletian where the face of the sun god is repeated in the metopes.

(Following pages) View of the house from the angle of the Northwest Terrace.

The two remaining outdoor rooms at the perimeter of the house are the Northeast Portico (the carriage entrance) adjoining the Entrance Hall, and the Southwest Portico adjoining the Parlor and overlooking the flower garden. Jefferson's plan for making these more livable spaces involved suspending louvered blinds between the Doric columns. The solution was particularly apt for the Southwest Portico, where the afternoon sun is intense. Jefferson considered several schemes, unfortunately none of them dated. The final idea appears to be for two folding blinds suspended between each pair of columns.[41] The lower half can be folded up and secured to the upper half by hooks, or both folded and raised to the ceiling. Nowhere, however, does Jefferson describe the pulley system necessary to raise and lower the blinds, nor has any physical or documentary evidence yet been found to prove that any were installed in either of the porticos. Furthermore, his mention of "Venetian blinds for the Porticos" in a September 24, 1804, list of work for his slave joiner John Hemings leaves it unclear whether Jefferson is referring to fabrication or installation.[42]

Four benches, each six feet long, were to furnish the Southwest Portico.[43] Although Jefferson does not specify their placement, one likely plan has two of the benches facing each other along the sides of the portico (between the rear and forward columns) and the other two benches positioned between the front columns and facing the house. This U-shaped arrangement leaves the area between the two middle columns open as a walkway. With the addition of louvered blinds, the portico would have been transformed into an inviting outdoor living room.

Jefferson planned to make the Southwest Portico a more livable space by providing benches and suspending folding louvered blinds between the Doric columns.

Very likely the two eight-foot-long benches planned for the Northeast Portico were to be placed along the open sides of the porch, facing each other as their modern versions do today.[44] But there is also an inventory, taken after Jefferson's death, that lists twenty-eight "black painted [Windsor] chairs" in the adjoining Entrance Hall. No doubt many of these were frequently moved outside.[45]

Both porticoes are connected to a spacious room by glass doors and triple-sash windows that function as doors. With the sashes raised and the doors open, the two worlds are wonderfully joined. The linkage is further suggested in the Entrance Hall by the floor and glossy floor cloth, both painted grass green at the suggestion of Gilbert Stuart.[46] Although it is easy to imagine Jefferson and his family and friends moving freely in and out of doors on a summer evening, we are told that this idyll was frequently marred by

> the swarms of impertinent gazers who, without introduction, permission or any ceremony whatever, thrust themselves into the most private of Mr. Jefferson's out-of-door resorts, and even into his house, and stared about as if they were at a public show …. When sitting in the shade of his porticoes to enjoy the coolness of the approaching evening, parties of men and women would sometimes approach within a dozen yards, and gaze at him point-blank until they had looked their fill, as they would have gazed on a lion in a menagerie.[47]

The visitor to Monticello in 1839, quoted at the head of this essay, arrived thirteen years too late to come and gaze at the great man and quiz him about his "monument of ingenious extravagance." Jefferson, who is reputed to have said, "Architecture is my delight,

Jefferson's design for Chinese-lattice benches for the "Porticos & terrasses" at Monticello.

and putting up, and pulling down, one of my favorite amusements," was well aware that what he created was subject to criticism.[48] In the fall of 1809 he wrote to Benjamin Henry Latrobe and invited him to come see his "essay in architecture." Thinking this accomplished architect might accept the offer, he apparently felt obliged to confess that his essay "has been so much subordinated to the law of convenience, & affected also by the circumstance of change in the original design, that it is liable to some unfavorable & just criticisms."[49] This "law of convenience" justifies the open-air living spaces at the perimeter of the house, which, by square footage alone, equal nearly half the area of the main-floor rooms. The fact that each space is slightly different is largely owing to its function and its relationship to the sun and prevailing wind. In breadth and openness the house goes far beyond the typical Virginia plantation dwelling that Jefferson would have known from his youth— houses recognized for their compactness and inward orientation. Monticello embraces the landscape and to a certain degree becomes part of it.

The shaded areas summarize the variety of open-air living spaces at the perimeter of the house. By square-footage alone, they equal nearly half the area of the first-floor rooms.

In a sense, at Monticello, Jefferson made permanent the experience of outdoor living that he described during the summer of 1793, when he rented a house on the Schuylkill River to escape from the yellow fever in Philadelphia. With him was his daughter Maria, then enrolled in school, who, Jefferson wrote: "passes two or three days in the week with me, under the trees, for I never go into the house but at the hour of bed. I never before knew the full value of trees. My house is entirely embosomed in high plane trees, with good grass below, & under them I breakfast, dine, write, read and receive my company."[50] Life under the trees ultimately found its venue on the porticoes, piazzas, and terraces of Monticello.

In breadth and openness the house goes far beyond the typical Virginia plantation dwelling that Jefferson would have known from his youth—houses recognized for their compactness and inward orientation. The porticoes, Venetian porches, piazzas, and terraces that comprise the open-air living spaces at the perimeter of the house (visible in part in the photograph to the left) show the extent to which Monticello embraces the landscape and, to a certain degree, becomes part of it.

(Following pages) The southwest (garden) front of Monticello from the fishpond.

Decoration
SIMPLE YET ELEGANT

RELYING PRIMARILY ON EXAMPLES FROM BOOKS, JEFFERSON produced drawings for many of the architectural details at Monticello. They were prepared for his joiners, principally James Dinsmore, assisted by two of Jefferson's slaves, John Hemings and Lewis.

The joiners were responsible for the finished woodwork and produced all the door casings, the base moldings, chair-rails, and entablatures required for each room. The primary exceptions to the use of wood were the frieze ornaments and other fine details, such as the egg and dart, rosettes, and acanthus leaves that were applied to the woodwork. These were made in Washington from a material called composition— a mixture of whiting, linseed oil, hide glue, and rosin, heated and pressed into molds. The exceptions are the sun-god faces made of lead for the North Piazza.

Jefferson chose the Roman architectural orders, exhibited in their hierarchy, as the basis of the "simple yet regular and elegant" decorative scheme noted by the duc de La Rochefoucauld-Liancourt. Palladio's version of the Tuscan order (the least elaborate of the orders) was chosen for the low-ceilinged rooms: the Library, Cabinet, and secondary bedrooms. The Dining Room, Tea Room, and the North Piazza represent three versions of the Doric, and the Entrance Hall and Jeffeon's chamber, two different examples of the Ionic. Palladio's Corinthian order (the most ornate of the orders used at Monticello) was reserved for the Parlor.

Even excluding most of the sashes, which were made at Philadelphia, and the doors, made at Richmond, the finished woodwork at Monticello took ten years to complete.

Jefferson's drawing of stair balusters for Monticello dates from the 1770s. In the colonies at that time, the usual form of baluster had a set of turnings that separated the column from the vase. Jefferson chose to simplify the form and merge the column and vase.

The entablature in the Dining Room is the same Doric form used on the exterior of the house except that the frieze is embellished with alternating ox sculls and rosettes.

The frieze ornaments for the Entrance Hall, Parlor, and Jefferson's Chamber are copied from Roman temples illustrated in Antoine Desgodetz's Édifices Antiques de Rome. The engraving (left) is from the Temple of Jupiter the Thunderer, and is the source for the Parlor. It depicts the symbols of sacrifice.

Jefferson, who once remarked that "Roman taste, genius, and magnificence excite ideas," turned to antiquity for inspiration in designing the dome at Monticello. His source was an illustration of the ancient Temple of Vesta—the most sacred shrine in Rome where Vestal Virgins tended a fire, symbolic of the hearth as the center of Roman life.

The geometry of the dome and the proposed method of construction are recorded in two pages of notes and in this drawing, both from Jefferson's building notebook.

Monticello's
Dome Room

Up a steep narrow stairway and halfway down an attic hallway is Jefferson's Dome Room, or as he sometimes called it, the Sky Room. There is nothing in the approach that would lead anyone to expect such a glorious space. Margaret Bayard Smith, visiting Jefferson in 1809, remarked that it was a "noble and beautiful apartment." She noted that it was not, however, furnished, nor was it used, "a great pity, as it might be made the most beautiful room in the house."

Jefferson's inspiration for the first dome on a house in America was the ancient Temple of Vesta at Rome. The room is filled with light and the walls brightly painted with a mars yellow distemper. The floor was originally painted green. Looking about, one sees the quirks that make the room so distinctive. The plan of the room is not a regular octagon; the circular windows facing the house are raised to the cornice and contain mirrored glass to hide the visible portions of the sloping roof. Then there are the enormous base moldings that seem arbitrary and out of context. But from Jefferson's notes one learns that they represent a classical parapet proportioned not to the room but to the overall height of the building.

The crowning feature is the oculus, the circular opening to the sky, four feet in diameter and twenty and one-half feet above the floor. To cover it Jefferson ordered glass fifty-four inches in diameter—about as large as could be blown at that time. The present installation of a single sheet of blown glass dates from 1989.

In one sense the interior of Monticello—like the Dome Room—is an essay in architectural juxtaposition. Startling effects are achieved by contrasting scale and by the intersection and even collision of moldings, all of which, when judged as independent features, appear to be proportioned rationally.

37

Monticello's Restoration

Although the Thomas Jefferson Memorial Foundation replaced the roof in 1924, one year after acquiring Monticello, serious restoration based on scholarship would not be undertaken for more than a decade.

THOUGH THE THOMAS JEFFERSON MEMORIAL FOUNDATION ACQUIRED AN aging Monticello in 1923, it was not until 1938 that attention turned to the kind of serious and scholarly restoration that has ever since marked the stewardship of this World Heritage site.

The driving force behind early restoration at Monticello was Fiske Kimball, a Jefferson scholar and Trustee of the Foundation, along with Milton L. Grigg, from the Charlottesville architectural firm of Grigg & Johnson. The first undertaking in 1938 was the rebuilding of the northwest dependencies, followed by the restoration of the southeast dependencies, including the South Pavilion, and the recreation of the gardens about the house, through the efforts of the Garden Club of Virginia aided by Edwin Morris Betts.

This scholarly vision of restoration was continued by Monticello Curator and Director James A. Bear, hired in 1955. Restoration during Bear's thirty-year career focused on the recreation of Jefferson's Grove, Orchard, and Vegetable Garden terrace, including the stone retaining wall and the Garden Pavilion, as well as the roads within the landscape.

Perhaps the most brilliant restoration occurred in 1991-92 under the leadership of Foundation President Daniel P. Jordan. Plagued by failing roofs, the Foundation faithfully restored what was probably for its time the most complex roof on a house in North America. Perhaps the boldest restoration to date was the installation of Venetian Porches—the louvered enclosures that flank the Greenhouse. For the first time in more than one hundred years, visitors are now able to experience the remarkable variety and quality of space that Jefferson created as part of his private suite.

The southeast wing of dependencies was restored in 1941.

Restoration during the period 1938–55 was directed by Fiske Kimball (right), chairman of the Foundation's restoration committee, and the architect Milton Grigg (left).

Documentary and archaeological evidence were the basis of the recreation of the Garden Pavilion in 1983.

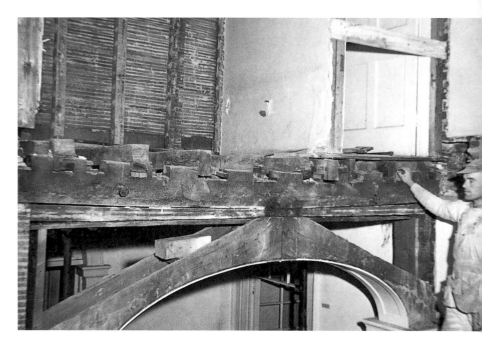

Stainless-steel shingles coated with tin were used in the 1992 restoration of the dome to replicate the appearance of Jefferson's tinned-iron shingles.

In 1953-54 a heating and air conditioning system was installed in the house and a major structural renovation undertaken. The first-floor level was reinforced from below with steel and the deteriorated and badly deflected second-floor joists were entirely removed (such as seen here in the Library) and replaced with steel. The original flooring was then carefully re-laid.

A Look Inside

MONTICELLO

Throughout his long political career in distant New York, Philadelphia, Paris, and Washington, Thomas Jefferson longed "to be liberated from the hated occupations of politics, and to sink into the bosom of my family, my farm, and my books."[1] Even while president, he came back to his beloved Monticello for two months or so during the heat of the summer while the government was in recess. After his retirement from the presidency and a lifetime of political service, Jefferson was at last able to return to Monticello. He was joined there by his daughter Martha and her husband Thomas Mann Randolph, Jr., and six of their eight children (three more were born later). Jefferson's mountaintop home became a hive of activity where relatives and friends might visit for weeks at a time.

Monticello was sometimes besieged with visitors, many of whom arrived without advance notice. Martha Jefferson Randolph, who managed the plantation household, complained to her daughter that they recently had "20 persons to dinner in the dining room and 11 children & boys in my sitting room 31 persons in all."[2] Even at Poplar Forest, Jefferson's plantation retreat, unannounced guests knocked on the door and were hospitably received. One of the granddaughters wrote her mother from Poplar Forest that "we had scarcely taken leave of one party, consisting of four N. Carolinians ...

by Susan R. Stein, Curator of Monticello

41

The House

Created in 1992, this watercolor rendered by artist G. B. McIntosh illustrates how Monticello's rooms might have been used in Jefferson's day.

Jefferson read, wrote letters, and studied the "tranquil pursuits of science" in his **Cabinet**

Jefferson awakened "in the morning as soon as he could see the hands of his clock" at the foot of his bed in his **Bed Chamber**

Jefferson grew plants and probably kept a workbench in the **Greenhouse**

Much of Jefferson's large library was kept in the locked **Book Room,** which was sometimes used by students

Martha Randolph, Jefferson's daughter, instructed her eleven children in the **Family Sitting Room**

Visitors arriving at Monticello were greeted in the **Entrance Hall**

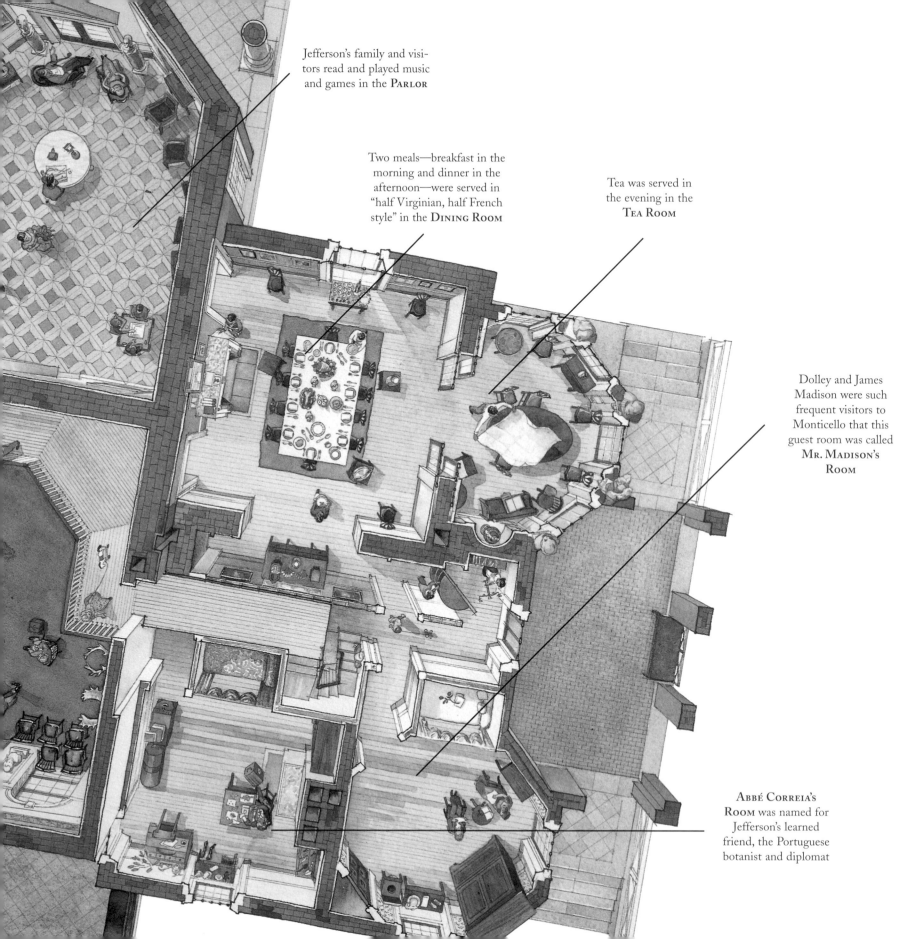

Jefferson's family and visitors read and played music and games in the **PARLOR**

Two meals—breakfast in the morning and dinner in the afternoon—were served in "half Virginian, half French style" in the **DINING ROOM**

Tea was served in the evening in the **TEA ROOM**

Dolley and James Madison were such frequent visitors to Monticello that this guest room was called **MR. MADISON'S ROOM**

ABBÉ CORREIA'S ROOM was named for Jefferson's learned friend, the Portuguese botanist and diplomat

when a coach and four, another carriage and a phaeton drove up to the door filled with ladies and gentlemen."[3]

When we consider Monticello today, our thoughts often turn, with good reason, first to Jefferson's remarkable architectural achievement and to his wide-ranging collection of paintings, sculpture, and the Native American artifacts he assembled within the house. The house, however, was more than a mere showpiece, as it set the scene for daily social and family life during Jefferson's lifetime. Jefferson's writings, family letters, and the accounts of visitors reveal a rich domestic life alive with activity. The sections that follow seek to illuminate that activity, suggesting not only how Monticello's rooms were arranged, but also how they were lived in during Jefferson's retirement.

Monticello's Entrance Hall served as a museum where Jefferson exhibited a wide range of objects that startled visitors with its breadth and variety. One visitor wrote of "the strange furniture of its walls" and the "curiosities which Lewis and Clark found in their wild and perilous expedition."

(Opposite) The interior face of the Great Clock, designed by Jefferson. Heavy cannonball-like weights power the clock and mark the day of the week as they descend from Sunday to Thursday, and then disappear through holes cut in the Entrance Hall floor. The markers for Friday and Saturday are located in the cellar.

Entrance Hall

Visitors to Monticello were enthralled by the Entrance Hall and the "strange furniture of the walls"—maps, antlers, sculpture, paintings, Native American artifacts, and minerals.[4] The atmosphere was markedly different from the houses of Virginia gentry, whose halls were typically hung with ancestral portraits. Jefferson regarded the double-storied Entrance Hall as a museum where he could educate his visitors while they waited to meet him or his family. After being received by Burwell Colbert, the slave houseman and butler, visitors might have rested in the twenty-eight Windsor chairs and taken notice, as did one visitor, of the "odd union" of "a fine painting of the Repentance of Saint Peter" with an Indian map on leather.[5] One visitor, welcomed by Jefferson, likened the Entrance Hall's "innumerable relics" to "the adornments of Romeo's apothecary shop where 'a tortoise hung, an alligator stuffed ....'"[6] Another noted that Jefferson himself showed guests a draft of the Declaration of Independence, "scored and scratched like a schoolboy's exercise." Visitors were struck not only by the unusual grass green color of the floor, suggested by artist Gilbert Stuart as Jefferson sat for his portrait in 1805, but especially by the double-faced Great Clock, which shows the second, minute, hour, and day of the week.

Parlor

Walking through the single-acting, double glass doors, some visitors were asked to enter the Parlor. The "large and lofty salon, or drawing room" described by the marquis de Chastellux was the principal social space where family members gathered and invited their guests to join them as they made music, read, played games, wrote letters, or took tea. One of the granddaughters, Virginia Randolph Trist, recalled the games that were played there. "When it grew too dark to read, in the half hour which passed before the candles came in, as we all sat round the fire, he [Jefferson] taught us several childish games, and would play them with us."[7] Conversation was an important social activity as well as an exchange of ideas. One visitor noted that "the ladies returned with the tea-tray a time before seven, and spent the evening with the gentle-

Family tradition suggests that Jefferson was a keen chess player. He taught the game to his granddaughter Ellen, and they sometimes played outside under the trees in the summertime. Jefferson owned several sets of chess pieces, including this English-style example.

men; which was always pleasant, for they are obviously accustomed to join in the conversation, however high the topic may be."[8]

The room was furnished for multiple uses and its movable furniture was configured to suit the activity and number of persons present. It was used daily as a sitting and music room and also hosted family weddings and christenings. A large number of different kinds of chairs and a sofa could accommodate family and visitors who assembled there in the late afternoon and early evening. The chairs were sometimes arranged in a circle for the Randolph children for reading and games. Jefferson's favored chair was a Campeachy, or siesta, chair in which he often read. Granddaughter Virginia wrote to her sister that a drawing of Monticello would soon reach her and that she "may even fancy … that you see Grand-papa's dear figure seated in one of the campeachy chairs drawn before the door for the sake of the pleasant evening air…."[9]

Sometimes visitors occupied the family all day long. In 1825, Mrs. Randolph wrote that they were "overwhelmed with company this summer" and that "people going to the Springs have us in the drawing room from 10 to 3, almost everyday."[10] A month later she complained again about the taxing burden of so many visitors, writing "to have a house constantly filled with visitors to be entertained in the day, and accomodate[d] at night, too often 'wears out welcome.' I am very fond of society but 'tou jours perdrix' is insufferable."[11]

Sometimes described as a "siesta chair," "lolling chair," or "hammock chair," Jefferson called this chair a "Campeachy hammock." He found the chair comfortable, writing, "Age, its infirmities & frequent illnesses have rendered indulgence in that easy kind of chair truly acceptable." Although Jefferson owned one Campeachy made in New Orleans, he also had several made by John Hemings, an enslaved joiner and cabinetmaker.

(Opposite) Surrounded by portraits of Columbus, Washington, Adams, and many others in the Parlor, the family played games, made music, and gathered in a circle to read. An Irish visitor noted that this room "during the summer is the one generally preferred by the family, on account of its being more airy and spacious than any other."

In the Dining Room family and guests gathered twice a day for breakfast and dinner. Visitors noted the books that Jefferson kept on the mantel to be read while guests and family gathered. Granddaughter Ellen Wayles Coolidge recalled, "In the dining room where, in winter, we passed a good deal of time, there was the low arm chair which he always occupied by the fire side, with his little round table still standing as when it held his book or his candle."

Dining Room

The Dining Room and adjacent Tea Room were important public rooms where visitors were entertained at breakfast, dinner, and tea. Jefferson's ardent interest in food and wine can be traced to his years in Paris; he recorded recipes—eight of which survive, including one for *biscuits de Savoye*. Monticello's kitchen had a series of French-trained chefs beginning with slave James Hemings, who accompanied Jefferson to France. Hemings was apprenticed to a caterer and then studied pastrymaking in Paris; he trained his brother Peter, who succeeded him. Peter, in turn, helped train Edith Fossett, whose cooking was praised by Daniel Webster after he visited in 1824. Webster commented, "Dinner is served half Virginian, half French style, in good taste and abundance."[12]

Monticello's kitchen, located among the dependencies, or work rooms, on the cellar level, was one of the best equipped in all of Virginia. In France, Jefferson purchased a large number of utensils, copper pots, and pans. Foodstuffs essential to fine cooking such as "macaroni, Parmesan cheese, figs of Marseilles, Brugnoles, raisins, almonds, mustard, Vinaigre d'Estragon, and other good vinegar, oil, and anchovies" were among the items shipped back from Europe with Jefferson's belongings in 1790. Once Jefferson returned to America, he obtained specialty items, sometimes from abroad, or from grocers in Richmond and Washington. The plentiful Monticello table was also the result of the variety of foods produced and preserved on the plantation. Mutton, pork, beef, and fish were served, and hundreds of varieties of vegetables and fruits were grown, such as

The Dining Room and Tea Room (above) were equipped with several dumbwaiters. These movable sets of shelves on casters could hold platters of food; they were placed between diners so that they could serve themselves. In the Dining Room (opposite), two small elevators, operated by pulleys and also called dumbwaiters, were built into the sides of the fireplace; each could lift a bottle of wine from the wine cellar directly below.

Dining Room. "We sat till near sun down at the table, where the dessert was succeeded by agreeable and instructive conversation in which every one seemed to wish and expect Mr. J. to take the chief part," remembered Margaret Bayard Smith of her visit in 1809.

(Background) A recipe for biscuits de Savoy, handwritten by Jefferson.

(Right) The silver tumbler today known as the Jefferson cup is one of a set of eight that Jefferson had made by silversmith John Letelier in Richmond. The cups were made in part from silver given to Jefferson by his friend and teacher, George Wythe. One visitor to Monticello wrote, "The drinking cups were of silver marked G.W. to T.J., the table liquors were beer and cider and after dinner wine."

This silver askos, a pouring vessel, was modeled after a Roman bronze askos that Jefferson saw in Nimes in 1787. Made by Philadelphia silversmiths Simmons and Alexander in 1801, it was dubbed "the silver duck" by family members, who used it as a chocolate pot.

cabbage, radishes, carrots, turnips, beets, peas, beans, kale, Jerusalem artichokes, asparagus, apples, berries, figs, peaches, and much more, including oregano, basil, and other herbs. Aside from Jefferson's gardens, Monticello's larder was supplemented by fish, poultry, and produce purchased from slaves who often had their own gardens and kept chickens.

Just two meals were served each day, breakfast and dinner. The breakfast bell rang at about eight o'clock. In 1809, Margaret Bayard Smith reported, "Our breakfast table was as large as our dinner table … we had tea, coffee, excellent muffins, hot wheat and corn bread, cold ham and butter …. Here indeed was the mode of living in general [of] that of a Virginia planter."[13] The Randolph children were so well behaved that "you would not know, if you would not see them, that a child was present," Mrs. Smith commented.[14]

A bell was rung to announce dinner, which was served in the late afternoon. The first summoning bell rang at three-thirty and the second at four o'clock. "The dinner was always choice," George Ticknor wrote, and "served in the French style."[15] Although many family recipes are known, no menus survive for meals at Monticello. However, one guest reported on the menu served at the President's House (now the White House) in 1802: "Rice soup, round of beef, turkey, mutton, ham, loin of veal, cutlets of mutton or veal, fried eggs, fried beef, a pie called macaroni …. Ice cream very good …; a dish somewhat like pudding covered with cream sauce—very fine. Many other jimcracks [nuts and sweetmeats], a great variety of fruit, plenty of wines, and good."[16]

Jefferson's own drinking and eating habits were moderate. His "breakfast is tea and coffee, bread always fresh from the oven, of which he does not seem afraid, with sometimes a light accompaniment of cold meat. Jefferson enjoys his dinner well, taking with his meat a large proportion of vegetables," Webster recalled.[17]

The presentation of dinner noticeably deviated from typical American gentry social practice, which required a servant or slave to serve each diner. Jefferson, eager to minimize the intrusion of servants, devised a more private and efficient system. A serving door with shelves was installed in the passage adjacent to the Dining Room so that platters of food might be placed on it from the passage and later withdrawn from the Dining Room. Jefferson also favored the use of dumbwaiters—sets of shelves on casters—which were placed between and behind the diners so that they could serve themselves. He apparently liked to serve his family and guests himself. Benjamin Henry Latrobe, the architect, observed at the President's House in Washington that "Jefferson said little at dinner besides attending to the filling of plates, which he did with great ease and grace for a philosopher, he became very talkative as soon as the cloth was removed."[18] Guests, including dignitaries, at the President's House and likely at Monticello were seated without regard to rank, or "pell-mell," from the French term *pêle-mêle*.

To serve food more efficiently as well as to enhance the privacy of the Dining Room, a revolving serving door with shelves was installed between the Dining Room and the north passage. Narrow stairs just across the passage lead down to the all-weather passageway, which connects the house to the kitchen.

Beer and cider were served with the meal but wine was not poured until the cloth was removed from the table after the main course. Wines from France, Spain, Portugal, Hungary, Germany, and Italy were served, though without the obligatory drinking of "healths," or toasts, as Jefferson believed that the practice encouraged people to drink more than they desired. Mrs. Smith took notice of his table "genteelly and plentifully spread, and his immense and costly variety of French and Italian wines, gave place to a Madeira and a sweet ladies' wine."[19]

While waiting for his family to congregate, Jefferson stood or sat and read in one of two small French armchairs that stood by the fireplace with a candle stand between them. One visitor noted that he saw "books of all kinds, Livy, Orosius, Edinburg Review, 1 vol. of Edgeworth's Moral Tales, etc." on the mantel.[20] Another person recalled that "she almost always found him reading, while he stood near the fire-place, waiting for the family and guests to assemble."[21]

A double set of glass pocket doors could be opened to make room for guests overflowing from the adjoining Dining Room, or closed to seal off the Tea Room, the coldest space of the house.

Tea Room

The Tea Room, what Jefferson called his "most honourable suite," was filled with portraits of friends, family members, and some of the people who had influenced him, including busts of Franklin, John Paul Jones, Lafayette, and Washington. When the number of guests at dinner exceeded the capacity of the Dining Room, the double pocket doors were slid open to create a single space. The Tea Room, on the north side, was the coldest spot in the house and contained a small iron stove to warm it.

The most conspicuous and unusual feature was a comfortable reading-and-writing arrangement for Jefferson. A revolving comb-back Windsor chair made in Philadelphia with an attached writing arm (added later by Monticello's joiners) was placed near a sofa or Windsor couch. Here Jefferson could stretch out his legs as he read or wrote. The sofa was used by others as well; a family account recalled granddaughter Virginia and a gentleman "setting very sociably side by side."[22] Ellen Coolidge remembered "the sofa where, in summer, I had so often sat by his [Jefferson's] side."[23]

Sitting Room

The Sitting Room was the principal private space occupied by the Randolphs and functioned as Mrs. Randolph's office and schoolroom. The education of her children was one of her main responsibilities. "My surviving daughter," Jefferson wrote, "the mother of many daughters as well as sons, has made their education the object of her life."[24] In addition to directing study of the classics, music, and drawing, Mrs. Randolph also instructed her daughters in domestic arts such as sewing. She was particularly determined to see that her daughters would be better prepared for housekeeping than she had been; each daughter took a turn as housekeeper for a month at a time, carrying the keys to locked storerooms, choosing menus, and more. As mistress of the sizable Monticello plantation, Mrs. Randolph directed the activities of the dozen slaves who were household servants in 1810.[25]

Margaret Bayard Smith recalled, "After breakfast … Mrs. Randolph withdrew to her nursery and excepting the hours housekeeping requires she devotes the rest to her children, whom she instructs." In the Sitting Room, family members played and worked, whether studying, sewing, or supervising the operations of the house.

Guest Rooms

The two first-floor guest chambers, located along the north passage, were named by the family for the prominent guests who frequently occupied them. The North Octagonal Room was dubbed "Mr. Madison's Room," for two of the most frequent visitors to Monticello, longtime friends James Madison and his wife Dolley. The room features a modern hand-blocked reproduction of the original trellis wallpaper purchased in France. Like many rooms on the first floor, the room also contains a triple-sash window which, when open, forms a doorway to allow easy access to the outside; interior shutters provide insulation and privacy. The bed is built into an alcove, a common feature of the bed chambers.

The Abbé José Correia da Serra (1750-1823), a Portuguese botanist, man of letters, and co-founder of the Academy of Science in Lisbon, visited Monticello seven times between 1812 and 1820 while he was Portugal's minister plenipotentiary to the United States. He was such a popular guest that the family called the space "Correia's Room." Jefferson wrote that he was "the best digest of science in books, men, and things that I have ever met with," and invited him to live at Monticello.

Two frequent visitors stood out for their popularity with Jefferson and his family. The North Octagonal Room (opposite) was known as "Mr. Madison's Room," and the North Square Room, "Correia's Room" (above).

Jefferson's Sanctum Sanctorum

A comfortable apartment consisting of four connected spaces—the Book Room, Greenhouse, Cabinet, and Bed Chamber—made up Jefferson's private domain. It was kept locked and was rarely entered, except by his daughter. Sir Augustus John Foster commented that "If the Library had been thrown open to his Guests, the President's Country House would have been as agreeable a Place to stay as any I know, but it was here he sat and wrote and he did not like of course to be disturbed by Visitors."[26] The Book Room was sufficiently private that washing its alabaster hanging lamp was considered "a Catch for Popularity"; Jefferson's granddaughters sought this chore to be near their grandfather.[27]

BOOK ROOM

In 1815 Jefferson wrote to John Adams "I cannot live without books."[28] He owned one of the largest private libraries (about seven thousand volumes) in America; it was "extensive and contains, as might indeed be expected, a vast collection of rare and valuable works, on all subjects, and in all languages."[29] Visitors, when admitted, were fascinated with the "valuable and curious books—those which contained fine prints etc.—… a vol[ume] of fine views of ancient villas around Rome … an old poem by Piers Plowman and printed some 250 years ago …. More than two hours passed most charmingly away."[30]

In addition to stacked open-faced boxes filled with books, "a little closet," made in Monticello's joinery, "contains all his garden seeds," Margaret Bayard Smith wrote. "They are all in little phials, labeled and hung on little hooks. Seeds such as peas, beans, etc., were in tin cannisters, but everything labeled and in the neatest order."[31]

According to George Ticknor in 1815, Jefferson's library "consists of about seven thousand volumes, contained in a suite of fine rooms, and is arranged in the catalogue, and on the shelves, according to the division and subdivisions of human learning by Lord Bacon." The Book Room (above) was part of an interconnected suite of Jefferson's private rooms, including the Cabinet (opposite).

Greenhouse

An inspired gardener, Jefferson kept flowers, plants, and flats for sprouting seeds in the Greenhouse. It was "divided from the other by glass compartments and doors; so that the view of the plants it contains, is unobstructed."[32] The Greenhouse also held an aviary, home to Jefferson's pet mockingbirds.

Jefferson also appears to have kept a chest of tools and workbench here. He had the skills to repair his scientific instruments and carry out "any little scheme of the moment in the way of furniture or experiment," a granddaughter recollected. Isaac Jefferson, a slave, remarked that Jefferson was "as neat a hand as you ever saw to make keys and locks and small chains, iron and brass."[33]

Margaret Bayard Smith apparently coined the often-quoted expression sanctum sanctorum: *"When we descended to the hall, he asked us to pass into the Library, or as I called it his sanctum sanctorum, where any other feet than his own seldom intrude. This suit of apartments … consists of 3 rooms for his library, one for his cabinet, one for his chamber, and a green house divided from the other by glass compartments and doors; so that the view of the plants it contains, is unobstructed."*

CABINET

In his Cabinet, or study, Jefferson was "surrounded by several hundred of his favourite authors … and every luxury and accommodation a student could require. This apartment opens into a green-house, and he is seldom without some geranium, or other plant beside him."[34] Satisfying Jefferson's "supreme delight" in the sciences, here were "mathematical instruments, mineralogical specimens, and the like, which indicated the varied intellectual tastes and pursuits of the proprietor."[35]

Alcove beds, enclosed by walls on three sides, are a common feature of the bed chambers at Monticello. The bed in Jefferson's suite, however, is open on both sides, linking his Bed Chamber and the Cabinet. A folding screen (now missing) was placed on the Cabinet side.

Correspondence occupied Jefferson for a large portion of every day. In retirement, the hardship of responding to all the letters he received tired him. He admitted to John Adams in 1817, "From sun-rise to one or two o'clock, and often from dinner to dark, I am drudging at the writing table." His letters—copied by a variety of polygraphs, or copying machines—were stored in five filing presses made in Monticello's own joinery, as well as in additional wooden cartons.

JEFFERSON'S BED CHAMBER

Daniel Webster reported that Jefferson's practice was to arise at dawn, "as soon as he can see the hands of his clock, which is directly opposite his bed," and then examine "the thermometer immediately, as he keeps a regular meteorological diary."[36] The black marble obelisk clock he designed and had made in Paris by Chantrot still sits on a shelf at the foot of his bed alcove; one of his several thermometers is placed on a nearby wall.

On July 4, 1826, the fiftieth anniversary of the day and time that Congress approved the Declaration of Independence, Jefferson died in his bed at nearly one o'clock in the afternoon. John Adams died later that same day, believing that Jefferson still survived.

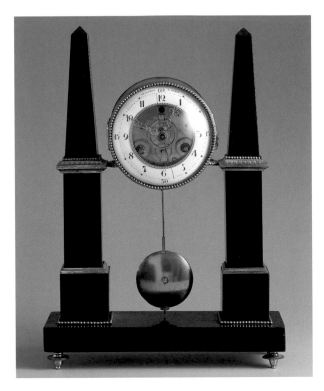

In December 1824, Daniel Webster
wrote, "Mr. Jefferson rises early in
the morning, as soon as he can see the
hands of his clock (which is directly
opposite his bed,) and examines his
thermometer immediately, as he keeps
a regular meteorological diary. He
employs himself chiefly in writing
till breakfast." Shown above is the
obelisk clock made by Chantrot in
Paris in 1790 to Jefferson's design.

Edmund Bacon, an overseer at Monticello, recalled, "He never had a servant make a fire in his room in the morning, or at any other time.... He always had a box filled with nice dry wood in his room, and when he wanted fire, he would open it and put on the wood." Another part of Jefferson's morning ritual was a cold footbath, a practice he maintained for sixty years and to which in part he attributed his good health.

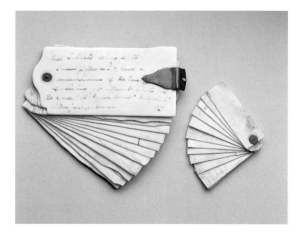

During his daily inspections of the plantation, Jefferson carried various portable instruments for making observations and measurements, including pocket-sized scales, drawing instruments, a thermometer, and a surveying compass. To record these measurements and other notes, Jefferson carried ivory notebooks on which he could write in pencil. At his writing table in his Cabinet, he later copied the information into any of seven books in which he kept records about his garden, farms, finances, and other concerns.

This English pocketknife, no doubt carried in Jefferson's coat pocket, has twelve tools, including saw, file, drill, corkscrew, and knife blades.

Inside Jefferson's pockets (clockwise from upper right): key ring and trunk key, gold toothpick, goose quill toothpick, pocket knife, ivory rule, watch fob, steel pocket scissors, and red-leather pocketbook.

The Second and Third Floors

The second and third floors were mainly occupied by the Randolph family, visiting relatives, and houseguests. On the second floor, six rooms opened onto the north and south passages and were heated by iron stoves. Four bed chambers echoed the plans of the rooms below, with two square rooms and two rooms with semioctagonal bows. A rectangular fifth room, above the South Piazza, was used for extra sleeping space, storage, and a nursery. The sixth and smallest of the chambers, directly above the Cabinet, was called the "Appendix" by the family, and provided extra sleeping space.

Two sets of narrow stairs, just two feet wide, provide the only access to the upper floors. Visitor Anna Thornton recalled, "When we went to bed we had to mount a little ladder of a staircase about 2 feet wide and very steep."

(Right) Margaret Bayard Smith wrote, "He afterwards took us to the drawing room 26 or 7 feet in diameter, in the dome. It is a noble and beautiful apartment, with 8 circular windows and a skylight. It was not furnished and being in the attic is not used, which I thought a great pity."

The Dome Room

In spite of its beauty, a visitor reported that the Dome Room or Sky Room "was abandoned by miscellaneous purposes" because of its inconvenience. The steep, narrow stairs made it difficult to reach. Crowned by an oculus of hand-blown glass, the room was painted mars yellow. Thomas Jefferson Randolph (called "Jeff" or "Jefferson") and his bride Jane Hollins Nicholas lived there briefly after their marriage in 1815. Two granddaughters made a hideaway

(they called it a "nice little cuddy") in the adjoining space above the portico. Grand-daughter Virginia recalled,

> *Cornelia's ingenuity in conjunction with mine formed steps from the dome into this little closet with a pile of boxes, and having furnished this apartment with a sopha to lounge upon, though alas! without cushions, a high and low chair and two small tables, one for my writing desk, the other for my books; and breathing through a broken pane of glass and some wide cracks in the floor; I have taken possession with the dirt daubers, wasps and humble [sic] bees.*[37]

After Jefferson's death, and possibly earlier, the Dome Room was used for storage.

The North and South Pavilions

Construction of the South Pavilion, believed to be the oldest brick building at Monticello, began in the late summer of 1770. Jefferson likely occupied it by November 1770 and brought his bride Martha Wayles Skelton Jefferson here in January 1772; their first child, Martha, was born in the building later that year. The Jeffersons lived in the South Pavilion—what Jefferson called the "outchamber"—while the main house was under construction.

In 1808, Jefferson stored his law books in the South Pavilion, and in 1809, Charles Bankhead, a grandson-in-law, studied law there. Later, the building was sometimes used for music and dancing.

The North Pavilion was completed in 1809 and, like the South Pavilion, is linked to the main house by L-shaped wooden terraces.

The lower level functioned as Monticello's kitchen until 1808, when it was remodeled as a washhouse, or laundry.

Completed by 1809, the North Pavilion was occupied by Thomas Mann Randolph, Jr., Jefferson's son-in-law, and used as a study. On April 9, 1819, sparks from the chimney ignited the wood shingle roof. Snow from the ice house prevented the spread of the fire to the terrace. Jefferson intended to use the lower level room as a bathing room, but his plan of "contriving a regular bath" apparently was never implemented. Instead, by 1823, a large tub was built for that purpose, but it is not known where it was placed. Both pavilions are linked to Monticello by L-shaped wooden terraces, under which are located the house's dependencies, or service rooms, including the kitchen, smokehouse, stables, dairy, storage cellars, ice house, ware room,

Overseer Edmund Bacon remembered, "Under the house and the terraces that surrounded it, were his cisterns, icehouse, cellar, kitchen, and rooms for all sorts of purposes." The south dependencies include the kitchen, cook's room, dairy, and smokehouse.

and some slave quarters. Above—and out of sight from—these workspaces, on the terraces, family and guests could walk in the evening, or sit on Windsor chairs or benches made to Jefferson's design. The porticoes and terraces enhanced the enjoyment of Monticello's landscape and gardens, in effect extending the living space of this busy house.

The terraces invited the family and guests outdoors. On the terraces and West Lawn, Virginia Jefferson Trist remembered that her siblings ran races, orchestrated and officiated by her grandfather. Jefferson himself was spotted walking the terraces regularly, whether alone early in the morning, or with family and friends late in the evening.

(Following pages) Northeastern front, or carriage entrance.

THE *Jefferson Family*
AT MONTICELLO

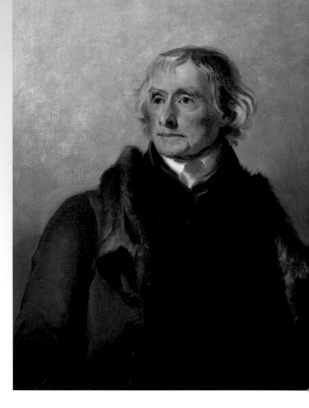

ALTHOUGH JEFFERSON'S WIFE MARTHA WAYLES SKELTON JEFFERSON DIED in 1782, he did not dwell alone at Monticello. Far from experiencing isolation, Jefferson lived with a wide gathering of family and an ever-changing array of visitors. At different times his widowed sister Martha Jefferson Carr and her six children lived at Monticello; his sister Anna Jefferson Marks also frequented the mountaintop. In addition, his daughters Martha Jefferson Randolph and Maria Jefferson Eppes were often at Monticello with their children. Following Jefferson's retirement from the presidency, his daughter Martha, together with her husband Thomas Mann Randolph, Jr., and their children made Monticello their home. As she had done during Jefferson's second term as president, Martha served as mistress of the plantation. After the death of Jefferson's daughter Maria in 1804, his grandson Francis Wayles Eppes frequently joined the crowd, prompting Jefferson to write to John Adams, "I live in the midst of my grandchildren."

—B.L.C.

Thomas Sully painted Jefferson's portrait at Monticello in 1821. "He is quite tall, six feet, one or two inches, face streaked and speckled with red, light grey eyes, white hair…," wrote Francis Calley Gray in 1815.

Martha Jefferson Randolph by Thomas Sully, 1834. Jefferson called her "the cherished companion of my early life, and nurse of my age."

Jefferson taught his granddaughter Cornelia to sketch and to paint. These are her box of watercolors and palette.

Jefferson Family Tree

Peter Jefferson 1708–1757 m. Jane Randolph 1720–1776	Jane 1740–1765	
	Mary 1741–1804	
	Thomas m. Martha W. Skelton 1743–1826 1748–1782	Martha m. Thomas M. Randolph 1772–1836 1768–1828
		Jane 1774–1775
		Son 1777–1777
		Maria m. John W. Eppes 1778–1804 1773–1823
	Elizabeth 1744–1774	
	Martha 1746–1811	Lucy E. 1780–1781
	Peter F. 1748–1748	Lucy E. 1782–1784
	Son 1750–1750	
	Lucy 1752–1810	
	Anna S. 1755–1828	
	Randolph 1755–1815	

Anne Cary 1791–1826
Thomas Jefferson 1792–1875
Ellen Wayles 1794–1795
Ellen Wayles 1796–1876
Cornelia Jefferson 1799–1871
Virginia Jefferson 1801–1882
Mary Jefferson 1803–1876
James Madison 1806–1834
Benjamin Franklin 1808–1871
Meriwether Lewis 1810–1837
Septimia Anne 1814–1887
George Wythe 1818–1867

Infant 1800–1800
Francis Wayles 1801–1881
Maria Jefferson 1804–1807

Cornelia Jefferson Randolph *(1799–1871) by William John Coffee, c. 1819.*

Anne Cary Randolph Bankhead *(1791–1826) by William John Coffee, c. 1819.*

Baby shoes worn by Jefferson's great-granddaughter. Proud of the size of his family, Jefferson wrote, "I have compared notes with Mr. Adams on the score of progeny, and find I am ahead of him, and think I am in a fair way to keep so. I have 10½ grandchildren, and 2¾ great-grand-children; and these fractions will ere long become units."

The women of Monticello spent a great deal of their time sewing. Among the objects atop the worktable made at Monticello are a needlecase and housewife (for storing sewing notions).

Born in Philaldelphia, Uriah Phillips Levy, a fifth-generation American, was one of the first Jews to serve in the United States Navy. He fought against the flogging of sailors and was awarded the rank of Commodore.

THE
Levy Family

MONTICELLO'S SURVIVAL IS A CREDIT TO THE EFFORTS of Uriah Philips Levy (1792-1862) and his nephew, Jefferson Monroe Levy (1852-1924). Before the historic preservation movement was even an idea in the United States, these men devoted themselves to the care of Monticello in tribute to the principles of Thomas Jefferson.

Jefferson Monroe Levy, a three-term United States congressman from New York, owned Monticello from 1879 until the Thomas Jefferson Memorial Foundation acquired it 1923.

Uriah Levy purchased Monticello in 1836 from James Barclay, whose attempt to turn Monticello into a silkworm farm failed. Levy dedicated himself to the preservation of Monticello, writing that the houses of great men should be preserved as "monuments to their glory." Levy died in 1862, bequeathing Monti-cello to the federal government. Political wrangling and tumult followed as the government rejected the bequest, the Confederacy seized control of the house during the Civil War, and Levy's heirs contested the will with lengthy litigation.

In 1879 Jefferson Monroe Levy, a successful businessman and later a con-

Monticello's Dining Room was embellished by fashionable furnishings of the late nineteenth century when the house was occupied by Jefferson Monroe Levy.

gressman from New York, purchased Monticello and used it as a summer estate for his family. In addition to maintaining the home and preserving it without major architectural changes, the Levy family also purchased a great deal of Jefferson-owned land and gathered available Jefferson-owned artifacts. Both Levys recognized Monticello's significance to all Americans, allowing visitors to tour the house and grounds.

*Jefferson Monroe Levy's sister, Amelia Mayhoff, with her son,
Monroe, on Monticello's West Lawn, c. 1900.*

*Jefferson Monroe Levy installed a French-
style bed in Jefferson's Bed Chamber.*

*The grave of Rachel Phillips Levy (1769–1839), mother of
Uriah Phillips Levy. At a ceremony in 1985, the grave site
on Mulberry Row was marked with a plaque describing the
contributions of the Levy family to the preservation of
Monticello.*

(In background) Monticello northeast front, c. 1870.

Furnishing Monticello

JEFFERSON AS CONSUMER AND COLLECTOR

THE WIDE ARRAY OF FURNISHINGS AND ART AT MONTICELLO REFLECTS NOT ONLY Thomas Jefferson's taste and interests but also his exceptional access to an increasing variety of consumer goods in America and Europe. Inspired first by what he learned in books and later by what he experienced firsthand in France, Jefferson aspired to join an educated international elite. Monticello's furnishings—its decorative arts, paintings, natural history specimens, scientific instruments, and Native American artifacts—very much expressed Jefferson's ambitious vision for his plantation home.

Jefferson's aspirations for Monticello required both unusual knowledge and energy; he looked beyond Virginia to inspire and to realize his goals. Monticello's complex neo-classical design, for example, required him to secure the involvement of skilled house joiners from distant places to construct the house. Likewise, Jefferson's cosmopolitan taste roused his interest in fashionable furnishings from Philadelphia, New York, and especially Paris. Charlottesville, a small town in rural central Virginia, was distant from the marketplaces of Richmond and Williamsburg, and Jefferson's excursions to urban centers became shopping expeditions. Like many planters of his day, Jefferson also

by Susan R. Stein, Curator of Monticello

ordered a variety of goods from makers as distant as London. At the end of his life, he turned to his own slave joiners to make a great deal of furniture for Monticello and Poplar Forest, his tobacco plantation and retreat in Bedford, Virginia.

Before Jefferson's journey to Europe in 1784 at the age of forty-one, his knowledge of the larger world was confined to America's eastern seaboard. He briefly toured Philadelphia in 1766 and lived there intermittently in 1775 and 1776 while a delegate to the Continental Congress. He lived in Williamsburg and frequented its shops. As a representative to the Confederation Congress, he resided in Annapolis in 1783 and 1784.

Jefferson in Paris

When he was appointed to serve as minister plenipotentiary in May of 1784, he made arrangements to travel to France with his oldest daughter Martha and two slaves, James and Robert Hemings. Jefferson sailed on the *Ceres* on July 5, arriving in Paris on August 6, 1784; his frame of reference—and Monticello's appearance—was forever altered by his experience there. The contrast between the great capital and the young cities of America was stunning. Upon arriving in Paris, Jefferson stayed in the Hôtel d'Orleans near the vibrant Palais Royal, an architectural arena that was much the center of the city's activity. The old palace had just been transformed by arcaded galleries containing six restaurants, a waxworks, a chess parlor, a theater and theatrical company, and galleries selling Old Masters, medals, and natural history specimens. Jefferson noted that the Palais Royal was "one of the principal ornaments to the city and increased the convenience of the inhabitants" while also bringing commercial success to its owners.[1] He clearly took notice of the consumer revolution that made a wide variety of products commonly available to an expanding middle and upper class. In fact, on his very first day in Paris he bought clothes for his daughter and lace ruffles for himself.[2]

Mr Jefferson

Ministre Plenipotentiaire

des Etats Unis d'Amerique.

*Porcelain decorated with sprigs of
cornflowers was popular in the late
eighteenth and early nineteenth
centuries. Among Jefferson's French
tablewares were a tureen and
other pieces, possibly made by
André et Cie, Foëscy.*

80

Eager to represent his country in a dignified manner, Jefferson sought accommodations befitting his ministerial rank and suggesting his place in a cultured circle of diplomats and *philosophes*. He hoped that his government would absorb his expenses, writing that "every other nation has established this" practice, but no reimbursement would ever be made to him.[3]

Jefferson's first real residence was a small *hôtel* (townhouse) on the cul-de-sac Taitbout in the Chaussée d'Antin. When he realized that he would remain in Paris longer than he had expected, he moved to larger quarters, a fine house designed by the architect Chalgrin at the corner of the Champs-Elysées and the rue de Berri. He outfitted his residences as well as he could at his own expense. In Paris he saw and frequented the *marchands merciers*, the shopkeepers who sold everything from fine silks and porcelain to furniture.[4] Most of the extensive purchases he made for his Parisian houses ultimately made their way to Monticello, where they contributed to its sophisticated

Tablespoons and forks in the common fiddle-and-thread pattern were among Jefferson's first purchases when he arrived in Paris in 1784. The monogram was added later.

character. His frequent entries in his personal account books, a detailed packing list of the belongings that followed him back to America in 1790, and many surviving artifacts give a good indication of Jefferson's taste and buying habits. If his tastes seemed extravagant by American standards, they were moderate when compared to the more lavish furniture, porcelain, silver, and silks prevalent in the dwellings of the French elite. Jefferson made his purchases carefully; he bought well but not opulently.

As Jefferson put together his household in a flurry of activity born of necessity, he first assembled the requisite items—linen for sheets and tablecloths, candlesticks, andirons, a coal grate, mattresses, blankets, stoves, carpets, kitchen utensils, lanterns, a coffee mill, silver-plated flatware, lamps and wicks, table wares, matches, and other necessities. On October 16, 1784, the same day that he signed a lease for the house on the cul-de-sac Taitbout, he paid 1,632 livres for "standing furniture."[5] The purchases that he made then would last him a lifetime.

Jefferson, Art Collector

Within three days, Jefferson was buying art for his house. He noted in his account book that on October 19 he purchased "2 small laughing busts, 2 pictures of heads, and 2 pictures half lengths, viz. An Ecce homo & another."[6]

Statuettes made of biscuit (unglazed soft porcelain) were popular table decorations. Of the six or more owned by Jefferson, only two survive, Venus with Cupid *(left)* and Hope with Cupid *(right).*

These were among the first acquisitions of what became a consequential collection. In all, Jefferson shipped sixty-three paintings back to America. Jefferson's purpose in collecting art in Paris was mainly didactic, but the choices he made were notably different from the desideratum that he compiled about 1771 for a projected art gallery at Monticello. His early list was primarily made up of classical works of art described in Joseph Spence's *Polymetis,* such as the *Medici Venus, Farnese Hercules, Apollo Belvedere,* and *Messenger pulling out a thorn.*[7] Jefferson's early interest in sculpture is borne out by two unfinished niches for sculpture at Monticello.

Jefferson's art collecting was undoubtedly influenced by the active artistic scene in Paris. The visual arts filled the biennial Salons, held for about one month beginning on August 25, the king's feast day, in the Salon Carré at the Louvre, where the latest works of the members of the Académie Royale de Peinture et Sculpture were exhibited. The landscapes, still lifes, genre scenes, portraits, and history paintings were hung frame to frame; history paintings ranked the highest in the well-established hierarchy. Although it is likely that Jefferson attended the Salons of 1785 and 1789, it is only known for certain that he viewed the Salon of 1787, and he was captivated by it.

Monticello's Parlor held more than fifty paintings; one visitor described the room as "hung with pictures from floor to ceiling." From Paris, Jefferson wrote James Madison, "You see I am an enthusiast on the subject of the arts. But it is an enthusiasm of which I am not ashamed, as it's object is to improve the taste of my countrymen …."

(Following pages) In addition to its remarkable collection of art, the Parlor featured an intricate parquet floor in beech and cherry, one of the first of its kind in America. Philadelphia upholsterer John Rea made the curtains at the windows following Jefferson's sketch and precise specifications.

Jefferson's collection of paintings included twenty-six presenting biblical themes, including Herodias Bearing the Head of St. John. *Jefferson owned this copy after the original by Guido Reni.*

He wrote John Trumbull, the painter, about the Salon's "treasures." "The best thing," he wrote, was "the Death of Socrates by David, and a superb one it is."[8] Jefferson's intuitive recognition of David's talent signaled not only Jefferson's growing sophistication, but also his preference for Neoclassicism. David's historical canvases and their ancient subjects appealed powerfully to Jefferson, who later observed, "I do not feel an interest in any pencil but that of David."[9]

Although the price of David's paintings prohibited Jefferson from buying them, he nonetheless put together a sizable art collection, largely of copies. Except for copies of five portraits from the Uffizi Gallery in Florence and five from collections in England, Jefferson acquired most of his collection in just six months between November 1784 and May 1785. He attended at least two sales of paintings, the De Billy sale in November 1784 and the sale of the collection of the late Dupille de Saint-Séverin in the Marais in February 1785. The sources of many purchases are not documented; the entries in his account book indicate that he usually bought more than one picture at a time, perhaps suggesting that his sources were shops or galleries. Of a total of twenty-one purchases, only three of the twenty-one sellers were named—two artists, Jean Valade and Mlle. Adélaïde Labille-Guiard, and Corneillon, from whom Jefferson bought engravings and perhaps paintings.

The paintings cost surprisingly little. Although Jefferson paid as much as 240 livres for an unidentified work by Mlle. Labille-Guiard, a portrait artist whose works were exhibited at the Salons, the average cost per picture was 29 livres, and some cost as little as 6 livres. At the time of purchase, Jefferson rarely noted the subjects, instead only noting "heads" or "half lengths." Most often he simply wrote "pictures," but later he prepared an inventory of the works he owned in which he identified the subject and the artist. Once retired from the presidency, Jefferson took time to annotate the "Catalogue of Paintings &c. at Monticello."

Jefferson's collection of copies favored Baroque artists, but Italian Renaissance paintings by Raphael *(Transfiguration* and *The Holy Family)*, Leonardo *(St. John the Baptist)*, Pordenone *(Christ before Pilate),* and Titian *(Danäe)* also were represented. Of the few surviving works, three Northern Renaissance paintings are now at Monticello— a copy of Jan Goessart *(Jesus in the Praetorium)*, a copy of Hendrick Goltzius *(Saint Jerome in Meditation)*, and one of the few original paintings, Frans Floris's *Descent from the Cross*. Baroque artists were better illustrated—Gerard Seghers, Antoine Coypel, Anthony van Dyk, Peter Paul Rubens, Francisco Solimena, José de Ribera, Jean Valentin de Bologne, Guido Reni, Eustache Le Sueur, and Domenchino Zampieri. The one artist that Jefferson clearly favored was Guido Reni; Jefferson owned copies of six of his works—*David with the Head of Goliath*, *Ecce Homo*, *John the Baptist*, *Herodias Bearing the Head of St. John* (which Jefferson identified as the work of Vouet), *Head of a Monk*, and *Christ*. The subjects of the paintings fell into three categories: biblical (twenty-six), classical (seven), and biographical (sixteen).

Jefferson acquired a total of twenty-three portraits between 1784 and 1789, including seven terra-cotta patinated plaster busts of Voltaire, Turgot, Franklin, Lafayette, Washington, John Paul Jones, and his own likeness by the eminent sculptor Jean-Antoine Houdon. All the portraits in Jefferson's collection depicted men whom Jefferson admired—the Enlightenment figures who provided the underpinnings of his values (Francis Bacon, Isaac Newton, and John Locke), the discoverers and explorers of America (Americus Vespucius, Christopher Columbus, Ferdinand Magellan, Hernando Cortez, and Sir Walter Raleigh), and contemporaries (Benjamin Franklin,

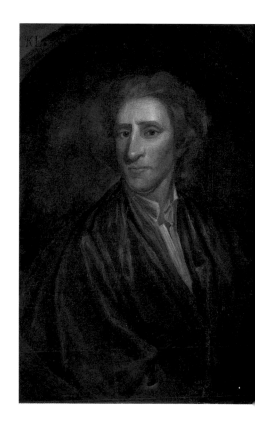

Portraiture was strongly represented in Jefferson's art collection, whether busts, engravings, or paintings. Jefferson called the Enlightenment thinkers Bacon, Newton, and Locke "my trinity of the three greatest men the world had ever produced." Of the three portraits, only Jefferson's 1789 copy of John Locke, copied after Sir Godfrey Kneller, survives.

the marquis de Lafayette, James Madison, George Washington, Thomas Paine, John Paul Jones, and others).

French Decorative Arts and Furniture

The art-filled interiors of the Parisian homes of the well-to-do also contained decorative arts that demonstrated the refined skills of their makers; Jefferson apparently admired what he had seen of the accomplished products of the silversmiths, *tapissiers*, and cabinetmakers. Jefferson's choice of a variety of silver wares, painted porcelain, biscuit figurines *(Hope with Cupid* and *Venus with Cupid* still survive), and candlesticks in the shape of Corinthian columns generally reflected his neoclassical taste. Jefferson himself designed a silver coffee urn and a pair of footed silver goblets; a small silver beaker with a gilt-washed interior inspired his later design for a larger version made in Richmond.

Jefferson's preference for simplicity met with further inspiration in the abundant seating furniture placed to accommodate the large-scale entertaining that filled the salons and dining room of the Hôtel de Langeac. Jefferson purchased twenty-two arm chairs, twenty-two side chairs, and four *bergères,* or easy chairs. A good deal of the furniture may have come from three *tapissiers-garnisseurs* who supplied household furniture to Jefferson in October 1784. The chairs were of at least five suites, each covered in different upholstery, which included bright pinkish-red, presumably silk damask; blue silk; red Morocco (goatskin); and two shades of *velours d'Utrecht,* a velvet with a pressed design.

The designs of the chairs varied. The simplest and most forward-looking were a large suite of mahogany *fauteuils à la reine*

Jefferson designed a pair of classically inspired silver and vermeil goblets which were made for him in Paris in 1789 by Claude-Nicolas Delanoy.

Among the chairs Jefferson purchased in France is a pair of fauteuils *typical of the Louis XVI period, possibly made by Jacques Upton. One of these chairs was the last chair in which Jefferson sat before he died. Immediately after his death on July 4, 1826, his grandson-in-law Nicholas Trist carved Jefferson's initials in the inside of the chair's left arm. The blue jasperware plaques made by Wedgwood may be replacements installed by Uriah Phillips Levy or Jefferson Monroe Levy.*

(armchairs with flat rectangular backs) with saber legs, attributed to the Parisian *ébéniste* Georges Jacob. The other suites were more conventional designs with decorative carving and painted finishes.

Other furniture at the Hôtel de Langeac included several gaming tables for cards and different kinds of games such as *jeu de main jaune*. For architectural drawing, Jefferson acquired what his packer Grevin called a *table à pupitre*, a table with a movable top, that eventually was placed in Jefferson's Cabinet and used as a drafting table. It was made by the cabinetmaker Denis Louis Ancellet, whose workshop was located on the rue Saint-Nicolas, although Jefferson seems to have purchased it from a merchant. A round marble *guéridon* (a table with a pedestal base) was so heavy that it was shipped back to America in two separate crates.

This mahogany fauteuil à la reine is attributed to the celebrated French cabinetmaker Georges Jacob. Monticello's collection includes eight of the original chairs in the suite, which may have numbered as many as twenty-one; seven are displayed in the Parlor. The desk with adjustable top is specifically designed for drawing, with the tabletop adjustable to the angle desired by the user. The sliding supports for the top have had extra notches cut into them to allow the top to be raised higher for Jefferson, who was six feet, two and one-half inches tall.

English Goods

In addition to art and decorative arts acquired in France, Jefferson's belongings included goods purchased during a trip to England during the early spring of 1786. He joined John Adams for a garden tour of country estates and also stayed in London to visit his old friends and to finalize a treaty with Portugal. Although Jefferson wrote Lafayette that he was not much disposed to English-made goods, he nonetheless purchased gloves, a hat, a walking stick, knives, maps, cotton stockings, and many scientific instruments. A year later Jefferson recalled the "splendor of their shops … is all that is worth seeing in London."[10]

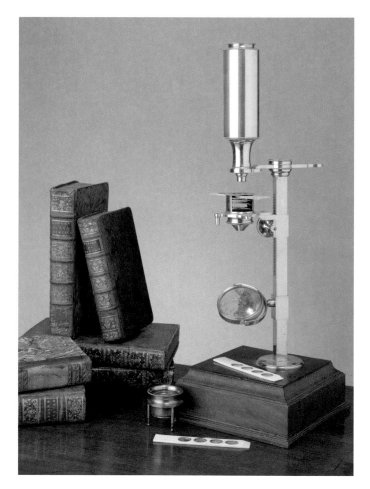

Jefferson, with his keen interest in astronomy, mathematics, and the physical sciences, particularly admired the English mechanical arts, which were "carried to a wonderful perfection."[11] He visited the shops of the finest makers and returned to France with an air pump, compound and solar microscopes, and his first achromatic telescope.[12] These were fine instruments, but not the most costly ornamented models. Jefferson's collection of scientific instruments included a portable orrery, an operating model of the solar system; a theodolite, a surveying instrument, with which he fixed the true meridian of Monticello; a hand magnifier, probably used to examine botanical specimens; a concave mirror for use with his microscopes; a micrometer; a surveying compass; an odometer for measuring distance; various thermometers, including one that he purchased on July 4, 1776, in Philadelphia; and more.

"I view no science with more partiality than natural history," wrote Jefferson in 1807. He read widely in the sciences, served as the head of the American Philosophical Society, and examined the world around him using an extensive collection of English scientific instruments including microscopes and a hand magnifier.

The scales and surveying compass shown here are examples of English–made instruments regularly used by Jefferson. These scales for weighing money and others he owned were vital to the careful management of his plantations. With his tools such as the compass below, Jefferson carefully measured his landholdings; his interest in surveying was prompted by his father, Peter Jefferson, a surveyor.

Return to America

When Jefferson's application for a leave of absence was granted on August 26, 1789, he waited nearly a month to depart for America. He fully expected to return to Paris, and he placed his secretary William Short in charge of his house and business while he was away. Jefferson sailed with two daughters and slaves James and Sally Hemings on the *Clermont* bound for Norfolk. Even aboard ship, Jefferson managed to make some purchases. He admired a London-made "Universal" table with two sliding leaves that could nearly double the table's total surface area, and asked the ship's captain to obtain two such tables in the "handsomest to be had" French spotted mahogany.[13]

Just as Jefferson landed at Norfolk on November 23, a fire broke out on the ship. Remarkably unharmed were the many parcels destined for Monticello containing dozens of bottles of French wines (Frontignans, Rochegudes, Sauternes, and Meursaults), vinegar, olive oil, raisins, books, a bust of Lafayette and a pedestal for it, mattresses, two bedsteads, a guitar, pictures, a clock, clothing, a phaeton, a harpsichord made by Jacob Kirckman, kitchen equipment, and more. The fire was not the only surprise. In Norfolk Jefferson learned that President Washington had nominated him to serve as secretary of state. Jefferson's time in Europe came to an abrupt end; before long he headed to New York to join the government in its temporary capital.

In New York, Jefferson rented a small house at 57 Maiden Lane. Apparently without hope that his French belongings would arrive quickly, Jefferson equipped his house with looking glasses, flatware, candlesticks from William

Jefferson ordered two of these London-made "Universal" tables while en route from Paris to Virginia. Also known as a "Secret Flap Table," the table has two sliding leaves that when opened, nearly double the area of the top, suitable for dining, writing, or drawing.

Jefferson's travel trunk might have contained his riding boots and socks as well as books, including petite format books, called octavos and duodecimos. He preferred the smaller books because they were cheaper, compact for traveling, and more easily handled with his wrist, dislocated in 1786.

Grigg; thirty green chairs, presumably Windsors, that would suffice until his French chairs arrived; bedsteads, china, and glassware from William Williams; and more. After Jefferson had lived in New York for barely three months, the government recessed and announced its move to Philadelphia.

Philadelphia

The house that Jefferson leased in Philadelphia at 274 Market Street was just a few blocks away from the American Philosophical Society, the State House, and his own offices at Eighth and Market Streets. When at last his possessions arrived from France, Jefferson paid "my monstrous bill of freight" for the shipment and storage of eighty-six crates; seventy-eight of them remained in Philadelphia while the others were shipped directly to Monticello.[14]

Unpacking was frightfully slow, but after weeks of effort the furniture was installed and the paintings hung. Despite the vast inventory of furniture, Jefferson was still not satisfied; he bought a bedstead from furniture maker John Aitken in January 1791. But Jefferson was not to remain on Market Street, for little more than two years later he decided to move to a country house near Gray's Ferry on the Schuylkill River. His "superfluous" furniture was sent to Monticello via Richmond in the spring of 1793. On December 31, 1793, Jefferson resigned his post as secretary of state, and returned to Monticello, "liberated from the hated occupation of politics."[15]

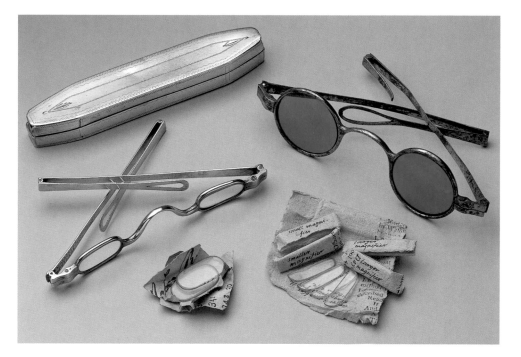

Jefferson designed the spectacles on the left, which came with lenses of varying magnification to accommodate his eyesight as it changed. The pair with tinted lenses were like others introduced early in the nineteenth century to improve vision outdoors.

Jefferson's full-time attention to his farms, family, and the expansion of Monticello was not long-lived. Public life intervened, and he found himself in Philadelphia again, this time as vice president. His presence there was intermittent, and during his first stay in March 1797 he found time to buy new gloves, a shaving brush, spectacles, and an oiled silk coat, and to make tentative arrangements to purchase a colossal bust of himself by the sculptor Giuseppe Ceracchi that he ultimately displayed in Monticello's Entrance Hall. Over the course of the next three years Jefferson would patronize the Philadelphia cabinetmaker Joseph Barry, who supplied standing furniture, most likely including ten extant shield-back chairs tentatively attributed to him. In 1801, the Philadelphia silversmiths Anthony Simmons and Samuel Alexander crafted for President Jefferson a silver askos from a wooden model of a Roman pouring vessel that he had admired in 1787 in Nîmes.

Martha Jefferson Randolph used this drop-leaf worktable, made in the Monticello joinery, for sewing. The drawers have a scratch bead at the top and bottom, a typical feature of Monticello joinery-made furniture, as is the astragal molding on the base.

Joinery Furniture

After Jefferson's financial resources considerably diminished following his retirement from the presidency, he turned to his slave joiners for furniture. These artisans, who had previously made architectural woodwork for the house at Monticello, produced an impressive group of furniture that included chairs, tables, and various case pieces, such as the seed press in the Book Room, a sewing table, the filing presses in the Cabinet, and dumbwaiters used in the Dining Room.[16]

Monticello as Museum

The enlargement of Monticello was largely completed by 1809, when Jefferson retired from the presidency. His belongings, a conglomeration of furniture, decorative arts, and various objects associated with his many activities and interests, were assembled in the finished house with an eye toward convenience and function. Monticello's interior became a highly idiosyncratic embodiment of his achievements, immense curiosity, and learning, as well as his life as a consumer.

Jefferson collected the best and most accurate maps throughout his lifetime, accumulating more than 350 different maps, navigational charts, and city plans. Eight or more large engraved wall maps and two Indian maps on leather shared wall space in the Entrance Hall with copies of Guido Reni's *David with the Head of Goliath*, *St. Jerome in Meditation*, and other paintings. To portray the natural history of North America, Jefferson exhibited specimens of many species, notably the antlers of the deer, moose, and elk, the stuffed head of an American argali (bighorn) sheep, and bones of the extinct mastodon.

Monticello Entrance Hall.
In 1816, Richard Rush, the son of
the famous doctor Benjamin Rush,
writes that Monticello was "decked
off with art and wealth," the "curious
assemblages of artificial or natural
objects forming quite a museum."

*Jefferson encouraged the American artist
John Trumbull to paint important scenes
of American history, including* The
Declaration of Independence.
*Trumbull began his great work in
Jefferson's house in Paris in 1786 but did
not complete it until 1820. The engraving
exhibited by Jefferson was made by Asher
B. Durand in 1823.*

*The fossilized jawbone of the American
mastodon, excavated by William Clark in
1806 in a dig at Big Bone Lick, Kentucky, was
also exhibited in the Entrance Hall. Jefferson
wrote about this rich ancient salt lick on the
Ohio River in his* Notes on the State
of Virginia.

*A profusion of sculpture, maps, natural history
specimens, old master paintings, and Native
American objects packed the walls of the
Entrance Hall. In 1818, visitor Salma Hale wrote,
"Mr. Jefferson I found on the top of his mountain
surrounded with curiosities, and
himself not the least …. His house is filled
with paintings and Indian relics, and a view
of his rooms affords as much gratification as
of a museum."*

Family tradition holds that these items, a figure, two heads, and a ceramic rattle or game ball containing small stones, belonged to Jefferson's collection of Native American objects at Monticello. Jefferson had a lifelong interest in Native American culture and gathered objects for the Entrance Hall from eastern as well as western tribes.

Jefferson's longtime study of Native Americans was realized in "an Indian Hall I am forming at Monticello."[17] In the Entrance Hall he displayed many artifacts of Native American culture and natural history specimens gathered by Lewis and Clark on their expedition, initiated by Jefferson, as well as other items he collected, including several earthenware figures, a pair of seated stone figures, and a kneeling woman, also carved in stone. The juxtaposition of western and Native American cultures was readily noticed by visitors; in 1815 George Ticknor commented that "in odd union with a fine painting of the Repentance of Saint Peter, is an Indian map on leather …."[18]

Sculpture, paintings, engravings, and drawings were principally displayed in the public rooms—the Entrance Hall, Parlor, Dining Room, and Tea Room. In addition to the natural history specimens, Native American artifacts, and maps, the Entrance Hall also exhibited eleven paintings. The Parlor contained no fewer than fifty-seven works of art and offered Jefferson another opportunity to instruct his visitors and family.

Among the pieces were thirty-five portraits of the men who had shaped Jefferson's intellectual development as well as American and world history. Their sitters ranged from the "trinity of the three greatest men the world has ever produced"—Francis Bacon, Isaac Newton, and John Locke—to Benjamin Franklin, George Washington, James Madison, John Adams, and David Rittenhouse, the brilliant Philadelphia scientist.[19]

The walls of the Dining Room and Tea Room were similarly crowded with pictures and portraits. The Dining Room held at least ten prints, eleven oil paintings, a watercolor, and three architectural drawings, hung in two tiers, and a plaster of a small sleeping Venus. The top tier exhibited two pictures of the Cynic philosopher Diogenes (412-323 B.C.)—*Diogenes in the Market of Athens*, copied after the painting by Peter Paul

Like the Parlor, the walls of the Dining Room were packed with prints and paintings, and also several architectural drawings. Although a copy of Raphael's Transfiguration *hung there, most of the pictures were American subjects such as Harper's Ferry, Mount Vernon, the port of New Orleans, and Niagara Falls.*

Rubens, and *Diogenes Visited by Alexander,* by an unidentified artist—as well as nine other paintings that Jefferson acquired in France. Of these, only Jefferson's copy of *The Holy Family* survives today.

The lower tier of the Dining Room pictures focused on American subjects. Among them were a painting by William Roberts, *Natural Bridge,* which Jefferson called "the most sublime of nature's works" in *Notes on the State of Virginia;* the engravings of *The Junction of the Potomac and Shenandoah, Virginia* and *Coalbrookdale Bridge;* and two views of Niagara Falls engraved after John Vanderlyn's paintings.[20]

The Tea Room, which Jefferson referred to as his "most honourable suite," was packed with portraits of patriots, friends, four Roman emperors, and family members. Four terra-cotta patinated busts of John Paul Jones, Franklin, Washington, and Lafayette, all by Houdon, dominated the space. A bust of Andrew Jackson, a gift, was added to the room in 1820. Sixteen miniature portraits included likenesses of Generals Gates, Dearborn, and Clinton; Meriwether Lewis; John Wayles Eppes, Jefferson's son-in-law; Albert Gallatin; William Burwell, Jefferson's secretary; Caesar Rodney, Gideon Granger, and Joseph Nicholson, political allies; and others.

Jefferson's private Cabinet contained all the accouterments associated with his scientific pursuits, and reading and writing—among them were telescopes, a tall case astronomical clock, the drawing table with a movable top brought from France, a writing table made in Monticello's joinery, a revolving chair, a revolving book stand, pens, drafting instruments, and a polygraph, a copying machine with which Jefferson made duplicates of his outgoing letters. After 1820, Jefferson set up a gallery of plaster busts of the first five presidents.

In 1774 Jefferson purchased Natural Bridge, located in Rockbridge County, Virginia, and enthused, "so beautiful an arch ... springing as it were, up to heaven, the rapture of the Spectacle is really indescribable!" This 1808 engraving after the painting by William Roberts hangs in the Monticello Dining Room.

(Opposite) Tea Room. John Edward Caldwell, a visitor in 1808, wrote, "in the bow of the dining room are busts of General Washington, Doctor Franklin, Marquis de Lafayette, and [John] Paul Jones, in plaister."

(Following pages) Monticello from the east.

Furniture

MADE AT MONTICELLO

A table with a revolving top, attributed to John Hemings, contains a hidden compartment beneath the top. The parquet pattern is similar to the floor of Monticello's Parlor.

IN ADDITION TO FURNITURE MADE BY cabinetmakers in European and American cities, Monticello featured furniture made on the plantation by a talented group of enslaved joiners. These artisans first produced architectural woodwork for Monticello itself and then turned to making furniture remarkable for its unusual design and construction. The chief joiner was John Hemings, a member of the noted enslaved Hemings family of artisans and house servants. Hemings, his co-worker Lewis, and other assistants worked in a shop on Mulberry Row called the joinery; it was extensively equipped with more than 125 individual planes, chisels, gouges, drawing knives, saws, a brace and bits for drilling holes, rasps, and files.

Although little documentation such as labels or marks exists to identify specific pieces of furniture, careful study has revealed about fifty works that can be attributed to Monticello's joinery. These include filing presses, tables, dumbwaiters, cupboards, a worktable, a seed press, and many chairs. The designs of these works reflect the influence of a variety of sources—principally Jefferson's own furniture from France, Virginia, Philadelphia, New York, and New Orleans—manipulated by Jefferson and his craftsmen in their own way. The resulting style, unusual for its French rather than English influence, has been called "Franco-Piedmont" by furniture historians.

A trestle table of mahogany is attributed to John Hemings. The marble top may have been one that Jefferson brought back from Paris.

(Left) Family tradition suggests that Jefferson had a role in making this narrow filing press and bookcase which was placed in his Bed Chamber.

Dumbwaiters, some made at Monticello and others from Philadelphia, were used in the Dining Room and Tea Room to ease meal service by limiting the intrusion of servants.

(In background) The designs for the furniture made in the joinery were probably Jefferson's, but only a few drawings survive, such as this plan for a worktable.

Five filing presses in the Cabinet contained Jefferson's vast correspondence.

The design of these tablet-back side chairs was likely derived from the Greek klismos. Jefferson probably saw a French interpretation of this form in Paris in the 1780s.

Reading and Writing

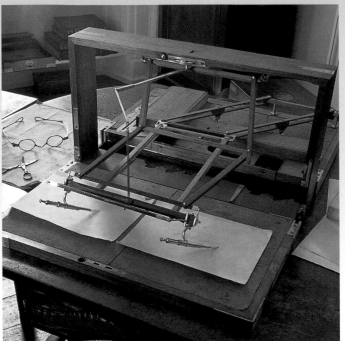

THE HEART OF JEFFERSON'S CABINET was his novel reading-and-writing arrangement, and correspondence was the principal occupation of Jefferson's day. Jefferson wrote almost twenty thousand letters in his lifetime, and he wrote John Adams that he suffered "under the persecution of letters," calculating that he received 1,267 letters in the year 1820. Surrounded by filing presses filled with letters and a sizable collection of scientific and drafting instruments, Jefferson sat in a whirligig or revolving chair, rested his legs on a Windsor couch with a tufted leather cushion, and wrote with a polygraph on a writing table with a revolving top.

Jefferson made copies of his correspondence using a polygraph, a device that he called "the finest invention of the present age." With this copy-machine, the writer moves one pen, and a second pen produces a duplicate letter. Jefferson acquired his first polygraph in March 1804, and five years later wrote "I could not…live without the polygraph." The use of this device and an earlier copying press has enabled the survival of much of Jefferson's vast correspondence.

An avid reader, Jefferson apparently liked to keep several books close at hand on a revolving bookstand placed near his chair. Likely Jefferson's own design and made in Monticello's joinery, the cube-shaped walnut bookstand has five adjustable rests for holding books at adjustable angles.

As he aged, Jefferson's wrist, which he broke while in France, troubled him considerably; he wrote John Adams that "crippled wrists and fingers make writing slow and laborious," even with the use of lead dumbbells and a wrist cushion, designed to strengthen and support his wrists. This copying machine, marked "Hawkins & Peale's Patent Polygraph No. 57," was used by Jefferson from 1806 until his death. Crafted of walnut, the revolving bookstand allowed Jefferson to consult multiple works at once, and may have been originally supported by a tripod base.

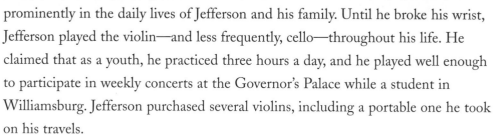

THOMAS JEFFERSON DECLARED that music "is the favorite passion of my soul," and music figured prominently in the daily lives of Jefferson and his family. Until he broke his wrist, Jefferson played the violin—and less frequently, cello—throughout his life. He claimed that as a youth, he practiced three hours a day, and he played well enough to participate in weekly concerts at the Governor's Palace while a student in Williamsburg. Jefferson purchased several violins, including a portable one he took on his travels.

Jefferson shared a love of music with his wife, Martha Wayles Skelton, for whom he purchased a pianoforte during their engagement, and he urged his young daughter Martha to practice music each day, writing, "Do not neglect your music. It will be a companion that will sweeten many hours of life." She played a superb harpsichord with a double set of keys made by Jacob Kirckman in 1786. By 1825 it was in poor condition, and one granddaughter wrote that "it was an old instrument too far gone even to learn on."

The family often gathered in the Parlor for "delightful recreation" after dinner. The family's music library, which was almost entirely secular, suggests that they enjoyed playing many kinds of music, from Scotch and Irish songs to works by Boccherini, Mozart, Clementi, Vivaldi, Corelli, and many more composers.

(Above) Among the keyboard instruments at Monticello was likely this pianoforte, or square piano, made by Astor and Company between 1799 and 1815. The cittern (above right), or English guitar, belonged to Jefferson's granddaughter, Virginia Randolph Trist. This harpsichord (right) made by Jacob Kirckman is similar to one that Jefferson gave to his daughter, Martha. However, her instrument had a double set of keys and a "Celestina stop" that added a bowed-string sound.

The Sciences

"MY SUPREME DELIGHT"

CLAIMING THAT "NATURE INTENDED ME FOR THE TRANQUIL PURSUITS of science, by rendering them my supreme delight," Jefferson read widely in the sciences, and corresponded frequently with enthusiasts worldwide. His Cabinet was filled with devices for observing, measuring, and recording nature. Influenced by Enlightenment thinkers like Sir Isaac Newton, Jefferson believed that a rational system of order governed the natural world, and that by applying these rules of science, the condition of man could be improved.

Fascinated with almost every aspect of science, Jefferson was particularly interested in those fields like astronomy, which were informed "by the aid of mathematical calculation," perhaps because he noted that "No two men can differ on a principle of trigonometry." As secretary of state, Jefferson established America's decimal system of currency, and argued unsuccessfully for the adoption of a decimal system of weights and measures. President of the American Philosophical Society for seventeen years and the only American of his time to be elected as a foreign associate of the Institute of France, Jefferson was known internationally as a man of learning. Today he is recognized, in the late Jefferson scholar Dumas Malone's words, "as an American pioneer in numerous branches of sciences, notably paleontology, ethnology, geography, and botany."   —B.L.C.

Jefferson's orrery, "an amazing mechanical representation of the solar system," was made by the London instrument maker William Jones.

A solar microscope projected an enlarged image of a tiny specimen such as the wing of a fly on to a wall or screen.

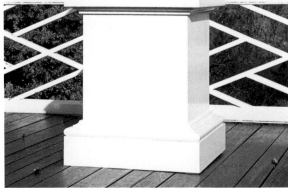

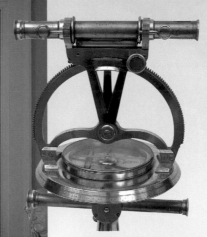

For surveying, fixing the true meridian of Monticello, and calculating the position of the features of the Monticello landscape, Jefferson used perhaps the most sophisticated instrument then available, a telescopic theodolite made by Jesse Ramsden.

Jefferson's fine collection of scientific instruments, housed in his Cabinet, enabled him to carry out a wide variety of observations, experiments, and calculations.

Jefferson claimed that his design for a spherical sundial was a "novelty" to him and that it "captivates every body foreign as well as home-bred, as a handsome object & accurate measurer of time." Installed in 2001, this recreation on the Northwest Terrace is based on his notes and drawings.

Jefferson is said to have used a telescope to watch the construction of the University of Virginia from Monticello's Northwest Terrace.

Jefferson owned several kinds of compasses, including this pocket-sized version.

The Gardens

OF MONTICELLO

And our own dear Monticello, where has nature spread so rich a mantle under the eye? mountains, forests, rocks, rivers. With what majesty do we there ride above the storms! How sublime to look down into the workhouse of nature, to see her clouds, hail, snow, rain, thunder, all fabricated at our feet! And the glorious Sun, when rising as if out of a distant water, just gilding the tops of the mountains, and giving life to all nature![1]

JEFFERSON TO MARIA COSWAY, 1786

THOMAS JEFFERSON'S INTEREST IN GARDENING AROSE FROM A WIDE-EYED CURIOSITY about the natural world. He chose the site for Monticello because of its sweeping prospects of the Piedmont Virginia countryside and its intimacy with the busy "workhouse of nature." The landscape was his "workhouse," and the gardens at Monticello became an experimental laboratory. Jefferson approached natural history as a scientist, as an experimenter who aspired to observe and define seemingly all the natural phenomena "fabricated at our feet"—whether the wind direction, the blooming dates of wildflowers, or the life cycle of a destructive insect. But it was through gardening that he could participate in the motions of this physical world—grafting peach wood or sowing cabbages

by Peter J. Hatch, Director of Gardens and Grounds at Monticello

113

with his granddaughters. Through horticulture his experiments bore fruit, his landscape assumed shape and form and color, and the drama of the natural world began to unfold under his personal direction.

Garden Scientist

Jefferson's methodical record-keeping reflects his view of the natural world as a biological laboratory. He has been described as the "father of weather observers" for his Weather Memorandum Book, a detailed account of the daily temperatures, rainfall, and wind direction. One of his most enduring legacies was his garden diary, published as *Thomas Jefferson's Garden Book* in 1944. This edition includes not only his personal Garden Book—a "Kalendar" of plantings in his garden, short treatises on soil preparation for grape vines, and meticulous notes on how many "grey snaps" would fill a pint jar—but also extracts from the letters he wrote and received concerning gardening,

(Opposite) The kitchen garden at Monticello was an Ellis Island of new and unusual vegetables, more than three hundred varieties from around the world. Scarlet-runner beans (Phaseolus coccineus), "arbor beans" to Jefferson, grow on poles along the "long grass walk," which is interrupted at its halfway point by the Garden Pavilion, reconstructed in 1984 based on archaeological excavations and Jefferson's notes on its design. Montalto, or "high mountain," originally part of the Monticello plantation, hovers in the distance.

Thomas Jefferson's Garden Book, which resides today at the Massachusetts Historical Society, documents Jefferson's horticultural career at Monticello between 1767 and 1824. It is a singular resource for early American plant introduction, landscape design, and fruit, vegetable, and ornamental gardening. The Garden Book is, among other things, a testament to Jefferson as a garden scientist: forever measuring, always meticulous, maddeningly methodical.

Monticello's flower borders come alive in late May with the blooming of (left to right) sweet peas (pink), foxglove (white), sweet William (mixed pink, red, and white), larkspur (blue), and Nicotiana *(white).*

natural history, and landscape design. Botany, agriculture, even surveying were essential to Jefferson's interest in horticulture and landscape design. An experienced draftsman and capable surveyor, Jefferson repeatedly measured his "Roundabout" roads and composed sketches of his estate. The woodland wildflower twinleaf, or *Jeffersonia diphylla*, was named in Jefferson's honor by the prominent Philadelphia botanist Benjamin Barton in 1792 at a meeting of the American Philosophical Society. Barton proclaimed that Jefferson's "knowledge of natural history … especially in botany and in zoology … is equalled by that of few persons in the United States."[2]

A close relative of the globe artichoke (and the thistle), Cardoon (Cynara cardunculus) *is cultivated for the stalks or thick stems of its leaves, which are often blanched, then sautéed in butter or cream, a popular feature of Italian cuisine.*

*(Below) Twinleaf (*Jeffersonia diphylla) *is a fitting tribute to Thomas Jefferson's interest in, and promotion of, natural history. Native to fertile woodlands along the Appalachian Mountain chain, twinleaf receives its common name from the bisected, or winged, shape of the leaves. Appropriately, the delicate white flowers appear around Jefferson's birthday on April 13.*

When Jefferson wrote, "The greatest service which can be rendered any country is to add a useful plant to its culture," he was expressing his hopes that the introduction of new economic plants could be a means of transforming American society.[3] The staggering number of both useful and ornamental plants grown at Monticello, including over 300 vegetable and 170 fruit varieties, attests to Jefferson's experimental approach. Monticello was a botanic garden of new and unusual introductions from around the world, and the geographic homes of the plants grown at Monticello reflect the reach of his gardening interests: new species discovered by the Lewis and Clark expedition like the snowberry bush and flowering currant, Italian peach and grape cultivars probably first grown in the New World by Jefferson himself, and giant cucumbers from Ohio twenty-four inches long. Thomas Jefferson envisioned plants as a vehicle for social change.

Jefferson also championed the use of native plants at a time when there were numerous European detractors of the American natural world. Georges Louis Leclerc de Buffon, in his *Histoire Naturelle*, argued that the New World's natural productions—its plants, animals, even native people—were inferior copies of Europe's. The only book

Jefferson organized the "winding walk" border into ten-foot-long sections, each planted with a different species or variety of herbaceous ornamental. Lavender, sweet peas, larkspur, sweet William, Nicotiana, *and corn poppies take the stage in late spring.*

Jefferson published during his lifetime, *Notes on the State of Virginia*, was partly an effort to refute Buffon's thesis that the excessive humidity in the United States crippled the biological environment.[4] When serving as minister to France between 1785 and 1789, Jefferson grew Indian corn in his Parisian garden and imported the seeds of American trees and flowers as gifts to his European friends.[5] Even in his ornamental plantings at Monticello, Jefferson created a pleasing blend of native and exotic plants. That he would refer to the tulip poplar and white oak as the "Juno and Jupiter of our groves" reflects his admiration for the spontaneous productions of his "workhouse of nature."[6] Presently, two massive tulip poplars straddle the west front of Monticello as a testament to Jefferson's appreciation of the natural productions of eastern North America.

American horticulture was in its infancy during Jefferson's lifetime, 1743–1826, and his association with the pioneer gardeners of the United States—nurserymen, writers, plant explorers, botanists, landscape designers, progressive agriculturists, experimental viticulturists—suggests Jefferson's vital participation in the definition of New World plants, gardens, and landscapes. Among his frequent correspondents was Bernard McMahon, curator of the Lewis and Clark expedition, nurseryman, and author of the best gardening book published in America in the first half of the nineteenth century, *The American Gardener's Calendar*, which has been described as Jefferson's horticultural "bible."[7] Furthermore, Jefferson's sponsorship of the Lewis and Clark expedition (which was, in part, considered a botanical exploration) and his role in cofounding both the Albemarle Agricultural Society and American Philosophical Society set a lofty standard for the promotion of scientific exploration by an American public servant.

"Humanized Horticulture"

For Jefferson, plants were intimately associated with people—friends, neighbors, political allies—and the exchange of seeds, bulbs, and fruit scions represented a token of enduring friendship. This union of gardening and sociability is evident throughout the letters in the Garden Book. Jefferson would chide his daughters and granddaughters for their inattention to the flower beds around the house, while they in turn would report on the latest horticultural dramas taking place at Monticello. Jefferson also engaged in friendly competitions with his neighbors to determine who could harvest the first English pea in spring. The winner then hosted a community dinner, sharing the winning dish (or teaspoon) of peas.[8]

Ellen Randolph Coolidge, Jefferson's granddaughter, recalled the heyday of flower gardening at Monticello: "When the flowers were in bloom, and we were in ecstasies over the rich purple and crimson, or pure white, or delicate lilac, or pale yellow of the blossoms, how he would sympathize in our admiration, or discuss … new groupings and combinations and contrasts. Oh, these were happy moments for us and for him."[9]

On April 18, 1810, Jefferson "sowed larkspurs" along his "winding walk" flower border.

(Following pages) The terraced kitchen garden was Jefferson's major horticultural achievement at Monticello. Supported by a massive stone wall, ornamented by the Garden Pavilion half-way along its one-thousand-foot length, and overlooking the six-acre Fruit Garden that included a propagation nursery (left) and the Southwest Vineyard (lower right), the "garden" functioned as an experimental laboratory. Both the Fruit and Vegetable Gardens were recreated in the early 1980s based on archaeological research and Jefferson's extensive records. The flowering dogwood in the middle of the Southwest Vineyard was preserved during the recreation.

The Garden Pavilion, perched precariously atop the garden wall, reputedly toppled over during a storm soon after Jefferson's death in 1826. A favorite haven for Jefferson to read in the cool of the evening, the pavilion was restored in 1984.

The gardens of Monticello hardly existed in a horticultural vacuum, but were nourished generously by a society of local, Virginian, American, and international gardeners.

Jefferson's essential philosophy of gardening was perhaps best summarized in a letter to his daughter Martha after she complained of insect-riddled plants in the Monticello Vegetable Garden: "We will try this winter to cover our garden with a heavy coating of manure. When earth is rich it bids defiance to droughts, yields in abundance, and of the best quality. I suspect that the insects which have harassed you have been encouraged by the feebleness of your plants; and that has been produced by the lean state of the soil."[10] Such commitment to the regenerative powers of soil improvement suggests Jefferson's belief in the wholesome balance of nature and gardening. His response to the damage inflicted by the Hessian fly on his wheat crop revealed more a naturalist's curiosity about an insect's life cycle than a farmer's quest for a successful harvest.[11] When Jefferson wrote that, for a gardener, "the failure of one thing is repaired by the success of another," he was expressing further this holistic approach to horticulture.[12]

In 1807 Jefferson wrote Timothy Matlack, a Pennsylvanian fruit grower, and asked for pears, peaches, and grapes. He added, "I shall be able to carry & plant them myself at Monticello where I shall then begin to occupy myself according to my own natural inclinations, which have been so long kept down by the history of our times."[13] The spring of 1807 was perhaps the most painful period of Jefferson's presidency as he suffered periodic migraine headaches that accompanied his involvement in the contentious Aaron Burr treason trial.[14] Even so, it was also the most ambitious and creative gardening period in Jefferson's horticultural career: the vineyards were revived with intensive plantings of twenty-four varieties of European grapes, and the oval flower beds were designed and planted. Gardening was a welcome retreat from the slings and arrows of political life.

Thomas Jefferson was a planter; 1,031 fruit trees were set out in his South Orchard alone. He documented the planting at Monticello of approximately 113 species of ornamental trees and 65 shrubs, over 100 species of herbaceous plants in his flower gardens, and 450 varieties of 95 species of fruits, vegetables, nuts, and herbs. The success or failure of his horticultural experiments was inconsequential compared to the example of his stewardship. Jefferson's enthusiasm often outstripped his practical capability; the saga of many horticultural projects, from grape culture to sugar maple plantations, began with dreamy visions that dissolved before the harsh realities of the Virginia climate and an unruly plantation structure. The history of gardening at Monticello is not so much a testament to Thomas Jefferson's horticultural triumphs as it is a reflection of the Jeffersonian spirit—expansive, optimistic, innocent, epicurean; very American.

Herbs, such as the lavender (Lavandula angustifolia) flowering above in early June, were included in Jefferson's 1794 memoradum "Objects for the Garden." The list included a variety of culinary and medicinal species that were likely distributed casually throughout the Vegetable Garden, rather than in a formally designed, discrete herb garden.

Landscape Design

In a letter to his granddaughter Ellen in 1805, Jefferson discussed the precise number of fine arts: "Many reckon but 5: painting, sculpture, architecture, music & poetry. To these some have added Oratory .... Others again add Gardening as a 7th fine art. Not horticulture, but the art of embellishing grounds by fancy."[15] Although his ideas on landscape evolved dramatically over his lifetime, Jefferson composed numerous fanciful schemes for the grounds of Monticello. He sketched over twenty designs for ornamental garden structures, some intended for the summit of Montalto ("high mountain"), which towers over Monticello ("little mountain") to the south. He also proposed a series of cascading waterfalls for Montalto and a classical grotto for the north spring at Monticello.[16] Most of these ambitious plans were never realized.

Jefferson's design from the 1770s for an observation tower for Montalto. The windows on the side facing Monticello were to be lower than on the back side so that the line of sight from Monticello would be directed through the building.

Jefferson toured English gardens in 1786 while serving as minister to France. He wrote upon his return, "the gardening in that country is the article in which it surpasses all the earth, I mean their pleasure gardening."[17] He was impressed by the newest landscape style in which garden designers attempted to imitate the picturesque schemes of eighteenth-century landscape painters and soften the distinctions between garden, park, and English countryside. This visit to England inspired many of Jefferson's ideas for the landscape at Monticello, including the planting of trees in clumps, the informal serpentine flower walk, and the Grove, or ornamental forest. It also stimulated Jefferson's unifying vision for the landscape—the creation of an ornamental farm, or *ferme ornée*.[18]

The Flower Gardens

The flowers come forth like the belles of the day, have their short reign of beauty and splendor, and retire, like them, to the more interesting office of reproducing their like. The Hyacinths and Tulips are off the stage, the Irises are giving place to the Belladonnas, as these will to the Tuberoses; as your mamma has done to you, my dear Anne, as you will do to the sisters of little John, and as I shall soon and cheerfully do to you all in wishing you a long, long, good night.[19]

—JEFFERSON TO ANNE CARY BANKHEAD, 1819

Although there were earlier references to the flower "borders," not until 1807 did Monticello's flower gardens assume their ultimate shape. Anticipating his retirement from the presidency, Jefferson sketched a plan for twenty oval-shaped flower beds in the four corners, or "angles," of the house. Each bed was planted with a different flower, most of which had been forwarded as seeds or bulbs from Philadelphia nurseryman Bernard

The "winding walk" flower border in early June. Jefferson wrote his granddaughter Anne on June 7, 1807: "I find that the limited number of our flower beds will too much restrain the variety of flowers in which we might wish to indulge, and therefore I have resumed an idea, which I had formerly entertained, of a winding walk surrounding the lawn before the house, with a narrow border of flowers on each side."

(Following pages) Monticello overseer Edmund Bacon recalled, "The grounds around the house were most beautifully ornamented with flowers and shrubbery. There were walks, and borders, and flowers, that I have never seen or heard of anywhere else. Some of them were in bloom from early in the spring until late in the winter."

Tulips bloom along oval beds and winding walk on West Lawn in late April. Jefferson wrote to Philadelphia nurseryman Bernard McMahon in 1811: "I have an extensive flower border, in which I am fond of placing handsome *plants or* fragrant. *Those of mere curiosity I do not aim at, having too many other cares to bestow more than a moderate attention to them." The Flower Gardens and fishpond (left) were restored with the help of the Garden Club of Virginia between 1939 and 1941.*

McMahon, a favorite source of gardening information for Jefferson. The range of flower species planted in 1807 reflected the scope of Jefferson's interests: Old World florists' flowers, local wildflowers, plants of curiosity, fruits of botanical exploration.[20]

In June of 1808 Jefferson sent his granddaughter Anne a plan for further plantings for the West Lawn: "I find that the limited number of our flower beds will too much restrain the variety of flowers in which we might wish to indulge, and therfore I have resumed an idea ... of a winding walk ... with a narrow border of flowers on each side. This would give abundant room for a great variety."[21] The winding walk and the accompanying flower border were laid out in the spring of 1808. By 1812, a need for a more systematic organization required the division of the borders into ten-foot sections, each numbered and planted with a different flower.[22]

The winding, relaxed lines of the walkway reflect Jefferson's interest in the latest, informal style of landscape design. The narrow flower border, or ribbon beds, chopped into ten-foot sections, would not be considered fashionable by modern standards, which celebrate the broad, mixed perennial border as the essence of garden art. The winding walk and border is not a traditional "garden," which usually suggests a room outside, an enclosed retreat. Jefferson's flower beds and borders are exposed to the elements, open to the Piedmont Virginia landscape, intimately balanced with "the workhouse of nature."

A year-round planting plan for the flower gardens has not survived; however, Jefferson would occasionally note specific plantings in the oval or "winding walk" beds in his Garden Book. Many eighteenth-century discoveries were forwarded from the Jardin

Tulip 'Apricot Beauty.' Jefferson wrote Madame de Tessé, a French friend, in 1803: "When I return to Monticello [from the Presidency] I believe I shall become a florist. The labours of the year, in that line, are repaid within the year, and death, which will be at my door, shall find me unembarrassed in long lived undertakings."

des Plantes in Paris, and nearly half the documented species planted at Monticello originated with McMahon. Twenty-five percent of the flowers documented at Monticello are North American natives, and the gardens became, in part, a museum of New World botanical novelties.

The flower gardens were cared for by Jefferson's daughters and granddaughters, often assisted by Monticello's most skilled African-American slave gardener, Wormley Hughes, or by Jefferson himself, who would help with the design schemes, write labels, or set up a string line to assure straight rows.[23] The flower gardens virtually disappeared after Jefferson's death in 1826, but were restored by The Garden Club of Virginia between 1939 and 1941. Working with Jefferson's sketches and taking cues from the bulbs that still bloomed 115 years after Jefferson's death, researchers discerned the outline of the winding walk by shining automobile headlights across the West Lawn at night.[24]

The Trees of Monticello

I never before knew the full value of trees. My house is entirely embosomed in high plane trees, with good grass below, & under them I breakfast, dine, write, read and receive my company. What would I not give that the trees planted nearest round the house at Monticello were full grown.[25]

—Jefferson to Martha Randolph (from Philadelphia), 1793

Jefferson undoubtedly ranked trees at the top of his list of favorite garden plants. Visitors to Monticello were often given tours of the grounds that included a rambling survey of what one guest described as Jefferson's "pet trees."[26] The image of lofty shade trees crowning the summit was consistently evoked by visitors to Monticello.[27] Even in his most functional plantings, Jefferson exploited the ornamental qualities of 160 species of trees.

*Jefferson wrote to Madame de Tessé, in 1803:
"I own my dear Madame, that I cannot but
admire your courage in undertaking now to
plant trees. It has always been my passion."*

He planted groves of native and exotic trees; "clumps" of ornamentals adjacent to the house; allées of mulberry and honey locust along his road network of "Roundabouts"; plantations of sugar maple and pecan; and living fences of peach and hawthorn.

While serving as minister to France between 1784 and 1789, Jefferson proudly distributed seeds of choice North American trees to friends in Europe, continuing a tradition begun with the earliest European explorers in the New World.[28] He has been described as "the father of American forestry" for an 1804 planting of white pine and hemlock.[29] His commitment to tree preservation was fervently expressed in comments he allegedly made during a dinner conversation at the President's House: "I wish I was a despot that I might save the noble, the beautiful trees that are daily falling sacrifice to the cupidity of their owners, or the necessity of the poor …. The unnecessary felling of a tree, perhaps the growth of centuries, seems to me a crime little short of murder."[30] Thomas Jefferson's enthusiasm for the arboreal world was unrelenting. Two months before his death, at the age of eighty-three, he designed an arboretum for the University of Virginia. He wrote, "Too old to plant trees for my own gratification I shall do it for posterity."[31]

Only two Jefferson-era trees have survived the inhospitable environment of mountaintop existence. These are a red cedar *(Juniperus virginiana)*, a species which, surprisingly, Jefferson said was introduced into Albemarle County, and an impressive tulip poplar *(Liriodendron tulipifera)* adjacent to the house.

Native dogwoods (Cornus florida) *and redbud* (Cercis canadensis) *in the Monticello woodlands. Anticipating his retirement from the presidency in 1809, Jefferson wrote, "Within a few days I shall bury myself in the groves of Monticello, and become a mere spectator of the passing events."*

(Opposite) Sugar maple (Acer saccharum) *along the South Terrace at Monticello. Sixty trees were planted at Monticello in 1791. Jefferson wrote, "What a blessing to substitute a sugar which requires only the labour of children, for that which it is said renders the slavery of the blacks necessary."*

The Vegetable Garden

I have lived temperately, eating little animal food, and that ... as a condiment for the vegetables,

which constitute my principal diet.[34]

—JEFFERSON TO VINE UTLEY, 1819

When Jefferson referred to his "garden," he, like most early Americans, was reserving the term for his thousand-foot-long Vegetable Garden terrace on the southeastern side of his "little mountain." This garden was his chief horticultural achievement at Monticello. Although the garden served as a food source for the family table, it also functioned as a laboratory where he experimented with seventy different species of vegetables. While Jefferson would grow as many as forty-six bean varieties and twenty-five types of English pea, his use of the scientific method selectively eliminated inferior sorts: "I am curious to select one or two of the best species or variety of every garden vegetable, and to reject all others from the garden to avoid the dangers of mixing."[35]

Sea kale plants (Crambe maritima) *producing seed. This perennial cabbage-like species, one of Jefferson's favorites, is native to the sea coast of Great Britain. As the growth emerges in early spring, sea kale pots are placed over the plants to blanch the young sprouts. When these shoots become eight to ten inches high, they are cut off at the ground and prepared, according to Jefferson, like asparagus.*

The garden evolved over many years, beginning in 1770 when crops were grown along the sloping contours of the hillside. Terracing was established by 1809, and by 1812 gardening was at its peak. African-American slaves leased by Jefferson from a Fredericksburg farmer hewed the terrace or garden plateau from the side of the mountain. They used a cart and a mule to level the terrace, which was described by one visitor as a "hanging garden."[36] The garden's dramatic setting is enhanced by the pavilion, used by Jefferson as a quiet retreat for evening reading. Reputedly blown down in a violent windstorm by the late 1820s, it was reconstructed in 1984 based upon Jefferson's notes and archaeological excavations.

The main part of the two-acre garden is divided into twenty-four "squares," or growing plots. Species were planted, at least in 1812, according to which part of the plant was being harvested—whether "fruits" (tomatoes, beans), "roots" (beets), or "leaves" (lettuce, cabbage). The site and situation of the garden enabled Jefferson to extend the growing season into the winter months and provided an amenable microclimate for tender vegetables such as the French artichoke and winter crops like spinach and endive. Because of favorable air drainage on a small mountaintop, late spring frosts are rare at Monticello and fall's first freeze rarely occurs before Thanksgiving. Jefferson would often gloat over his lowland neighbors' loss of frostbitten fruit, while his own remained unscathed.

Aside from the Garden Pavilion, Jefferson occasionally considered other ornamental features for the terrace. He discussed planting an arbor of different flowering shades of the scarlet runner bean ("purple, red, scarlet, and white"), arranged adjacent rows of purple, white, and green sprouting broccoli, or even white and purple eggplant, and he bordered his tomato square with sesame or okra, a rather unusual juxtaposition of plant textures. Cherry trees were also planted along the "long, grass walk," at the edge of the garden above the wall, to provide shade and spring flowers.[37]

Hyacinth bean (Dolichos lablab) *flowers are a visual highlight in the garden late in summer.*

(Opposite) Jefferson wrote in his Garden Book on April 17, 1811: "Arbor beans white, scarlet, crimson, purple … on long walk of garden." The recreated wooden arbor, made from the forked limbs of black locust, is based on a Jefferson design for a grape arbor and covers the southwestern end of the "long walk."

Salads were an important part of Jefferson's diet. He would note the planting of lettuce and radishes every two weeks through the growing season; grow interesting greens like orach, corn salad, endive, and nasturtiums; and plant sesame in order to manufacture a suitable salad oil. While the English pea is considered his favorite vegetable, he also cherished figs, asparagus, artichokes, and such "new" vegetables as tomatoes, eggplant, broccoli, and cauliflower. While Jefferson cultivated common crops like cucumbers, cabbages, and beans, he also prized his sea kale *(Crambe maritima)*, a perennial cabbagelike species whose spring sprouts were blanched with pots, then cut and prepared like asparagus. The cultural directions in Bernard McMahon's *Calendar*—for manuring the garden, interplanting lettuce and radishes, and planting cucumbers in hogsheads—were followed diligently in the Monticello garden. McMahon also sent Jefferson important vegetable vari-

eties such as Leadman's Dwarf pea, Egyptian onion, Early York and Sugarloaf cabbage, red celery, and red globe artichoke.

Jefferson's meticulous notes on the day when peas were sowed or beans harvested suggest he was an active participant in the gardening process. Years after Jefferson's death, one of his former slaves, Isaac Jefferson, recalled, "For amusement he would work sometimes in the garden for half an hour at a time in the cool of the evening."[38] Margaret Bayard Smith, a friend of Jefferson's and a visitor to Monticello, described a portable "frame, or stand, consisting of two upright pieces of about two inches thickness, in which were neat little truss hooks. On these were suspended phials of all sizes, tightly corked, and neatly labelled, containing garden seeds. When in his garden this stand could be carried about and placed near him, and if I remember, there must have been near a hundred kinds."[39] Apparently, Jefferson regularly planted the garden himself; however, he was aided

Tree, or Egyptian, onions were planted by Jefferson on April 11, 1809. His attention to detail was expressed in his Garden Book planting notes: "of these seed bulbs, 111 fill a pint. To plant a square of 40.f in drills 12.I. apart & 4 I. in the drill will take 5 ½ gallons, say 3. pecks." This unique type of onion produces edible (and plantable) bulbs above, as well as below, the ground.

(Right) The garden in early summer. Jefferson wrote Charles Willson Peale in 1811, "I have often thought that if heaven had given me choice of my position and calling, it should have been on a rich spot of earth, well watered, and near a good market for the productions of the garden."

by elderly slaves sometimes referred to as the "veteran aids,"[40] who in turn were often led by a series of African-American head gardeners: Goliah; Gardener John, who also tended grapes and planted trees that survived well into the second half of the twentieth century; and Great George, who later became Monticello's only African-American overseer.

The recreation of the Monticello Vegetable Garden began in 1979 with two years of archaeological excavations designed to confirm details from the documentary evidence. Archaeologists uncovered the remnants of the stone wall, exposed the foundation of the Garden Pavilion, and discovered evidence for the location of the entrance gate, which then ensured that the squares were laid out according to Jefferson's specifications. Harvested vegetables are today distributed to Monticello employees; in addition, the garden serves as a preservation seed bank of Jeffersonian and nineteenth-century vegetable varieties.

Fruit Garden

Monticello's Fruit Garden, or "Fruitery" as Jefferson called it in 1814, sprawls below the Vegetable Garden. It includes the four-hundred-tree South Orchard; two small vineyards ("northeast" and "southwest"); berry squares of currants, gooseberries, and raspberries; a nursery where Jefferson propagated fruit trees and special garden plants; and "submural beds," where figs and strawberries were grown

The Hewes' Crab, the most popular apple in eighteenth-century Virginia, was an important cider apple at Monticello.

to take advantage of the warming microclimate created by the stone wall. On the other side of the mountain, Jefferson's North Orchard was reserved for cider apples and seedling peaches (peach trees grown from seed).

Both the Monticello Fruitery (including the South Orchard) and the North Orchard reflected the two distinct forms of fruit growing in eighteenth-century Virginia.

The North Orchard was typical of the "field" or "farm" orchards found on most middle-class farms: it was large, on average two hundred trees, and consisted of only apple or peach trees. The fruit was harvested for cider, brandy, or as livestock feed. There is some truth to one historian's tongue-in-cheek remark that it was a significant event when Americans began eating their fruit rather than drinking it.[41] On the other hand, the Monticello Fruitery resembled a gentleman's fruit garden in the Old World horticultural tradition, and was similar to the diverse recreational plantings of other wealthy Virginians such as George Washington. The trees, often planted with small fruits and even ornamentals, were grafted and included a wide spectrum of European varieties and unusual species like apricots and almonds, reserved, according to Jefferson, for the "precious refreshment" of their fancy fruit.[42] The Fruit Garden was cared for sporadically by a series of itinerant European horticulturists, including Scotsman Robert Bailey and Italian Anthony Giannini. They were aided, at least at times, by enslaved African Americans like Great George and Gardener John, who espaliered grapes while Jefferson was in Europe.[43]

NURSERIES

Jefferson had at least two nurseries: the "old nursery" below the garden wall and the terraced "new nursery," which was an extension of the northeast end of the Vegetable Garden. Here he and Wormley Hughes propagated seeds and cuttings from friends and neighbors. The list of plants grown in the Monticello nurseries included Jefferson's favorite species: thirteen kinds of shrubs, forty-one species of ornamental trees, twenty-six vegetable varieties, six kinds of grasses, eleven nut trees, and fifty-three fruit tree varieties. They were the heart of his pomological, if not horticultural, world. In 1994, a nursery exhibit was recreated on the site of the "old nursery."

Flowers of the Violet Hative, the oldest nectarine variety still in cultivation, below the fence that surrounds what Jefferson referred to as the "old nursery." The South Orchard exists today as a repository of Jefferson-era fruit varieties, many of which are propagated in the nursery.

Sweet cherry trees bloom in the South Orchard below the garden wall. Cherry trees were commonly planted as ornamentals in the eighteenth and nineteenth centuries, and at least six trees grew along the "long walk" of the Vegetable Garden.

FENCES

The Fruitery (as well as the Vegetable Garden) was enclosed with a variety of materials during Jefferson's fruit-growing career: board fences, living hawthorn hedges, and even ditches that functioned as cattle guards. The most ambitious enclosure was the paling fence, built by a white carpenter, Mr. Watkins, and three enslaved African Americans in 1808 and 1809. Ten feet high, the fence extended nearly three-quarters of a mile around the entire complex. The palings, or thin boards, were "so near as not to let even a young hare in."[44] Although the paling gates were secured with a lock and key, overseer Edmund Bacon recalled fruit fights that arose when a band of schoolboys, rivals to Jefferson's grandson Thomas Jefferson Randolph, broke down the palings and "did a great deal of damage" by pelting each other with unripe apples and peaches.[45] Although most nineteenth-century orchards were fenced, it was customary for travelers through the Virginia countryside to help themselves to bearing fruit.[46] A sample of the paling fence has been recreated along Mulberry Row.

THE SOUTH ORCHARD

Between 1769 and 1814, the South Orchard was planted with as many as 1,031 fruit trees. It was organized into a grid pattern in which grew eighteen varieties of apple, thirty-eight of peach, fourteen cherry, twelve pear, twenty-seven plum, four nectarine, seven almond, six apricot, and one quince tree. The earliest plantings, before 1780, reflect the experimental orchard of a young Thomas Jefferson eager to import Mediterranean culture to Virginia and included olives, almonds, pomegranates, and figs. The mature plantings, after 1810, included mostly species and varieties that thrived through central Virginia's hot, humid summers and cold, rainy winters—such as seedling peaches and Virginia cider apples—or else, Jefferson's favorite fancy fruits like the Carnation cherry. The restoration of the South Orchard began in 1981 and was an attempt to recreate his mature, 1811 plan.[47]

Fruits of the Royal George peach, an eighteenth-century European variety. Jefferson mentioned the planting of thirty-seven varieties of peach, which, based on the quantity of trees set out at Monticello, could be considered his favorite kind of fruit.

The peach might be regarded as Jefferson's favorite type of fruit tree; he documented the planting of 38 varieties, and in 1811 the South Orchard included 160 peach trees, far more than any other species. When Jefferson wrote his granddaughter in 1815 that "we abound in the luxury of peach,"[48] he was repeating a theme expressed by colonial fruit growers and even the first natural historians of the New World. At Monticello, peaches were commonly dried and also made into mobby, a form of brandy; in addition, peach

African–American Gardens
AT MONTICELLO

AIDED BY HIS DAUGHTERS AND GRANDDAUGHTERS, ITINERANT EUROPEAN GARDENERS, and enslaved workers, from the young to the "veteran aids," Thomas Jefferson did not garden alone at Monticello. But just as Jefferson was not the only gardener, so were the mountaintop Flower, Fruit, and Vegetable Gardens not the only gardens at Monticello.

Jefferson's Memorandum Books and a family account ledger document the purchase of twenty-two species of fruits and vegetables from as many as forty-three Monticello and neighboring slaves. Many of the slaves involved in the transactions, presumably bartering over the price of twenty-five cabbages or a "mess" of greens, were probably representing family gardens. Squire, for example, sold thirteen different types of vegetables, including a cucumber sold to Jefferson in the middle of the winter of 1773. Bagwell, Squire's son-in-law, sold Jefferson sixty pounds of hops for twenty dollars, perhaps from the same garden. Many of the produce purchases were out of season: potatoes sold in December and February, hominy beans and apples purchased in April, and cucumbers bought in January. Archaeological excavations of slave cabins at Monticello indicate the presence of root cellars, which not only served as secret hiding places for precious items, but surely, as repositories for root crops and other vegetables amenable to cool, dark storage. Produce from slave gardens at Monticello seemed to be purposefully directed toward the out-of-season table and included garden staples like cucumbers, cabbages, and potatoes.

The African-American gardens were likely associated with quarter-farm communities or isolated cabins on the five-thousand-acre Monticello plantation. Work in these gardens took place on Sundays or at night after slaves were excused from their field or day's labor. One oral tradition suggests that garden work was illuminated by lighting animal fat in cast iron pots and pans. Cucumbers were the most common commodity, followed by cabbages, watermelons, hops, Irish potatoes, patty-pan squash, and greens. These gardens suggest the vitality and entrepreneurial spirit of the Monticello African-American community and the beginnings of an African-American horticultural tradition.

Jefferson's Memorandum Books document the purchase of over twenty-two species of fruits and vegetables from Monticello slaves. The transactions in this family ledger were recorded by granddaughter Anne Cary Randolph.

Cabbages ranked second among vegetables commonly sold to the Jefferson family.

(Left) Cymlins, or patty pan squash, were among the vegetables sold to the Jefferson family by Monticello slaves. The African-American gardens primarily provided produce for everyday use at the table.

THE THOMAS JEFFERSON CENTER FOR
Historic Plants

A FITTING TRIBUTE TO JEFFERSON'S INTEREST IN GARDEN PLANTS, AND THE natural result of the restoration of Jefferson's gardens at Monticello, was the opening of the Thomas Jefferson Center for Historic Plants in 1987. The Center is an educational garden center devoted to the collection, preservation, and distribution of plants known in early American gardens. The program centers on Thomas Jefferson's horticultural interests and the plants he grew at Monticello, but covers the broad history of plants cultivated in America by including varieties documented through the nineteenth century, as well as choice North American plants, a group of special interest to Jefferson himself. The Garden Shop, open from March to November, is located at the Monticello Shuttle Parking Area. Historic plants, heirloom seeds, and books on the history of garden plants are available through the Shop. A newsletter, *Twinleaf*, chronicles the Center's work and includes a mail-order catalog of seeds and plants from Monticello. The Center's Nursery, at nearby Tufton Farm, includes growing facilities and display gardens for its collection of historic roses, Dianthus, and iris.

Globe centaurea (Centaurea macrocephala) *was among the uncommon perennials sent to Monticello by Philadelphia nurseryman Bernard McMahon in 1812.*

Maltese cross (Lychnis chalcedonica) *was planted in an oval flower bed in April 1807. The Center for Historic Plants has a large collection of historic varieties and species of herbaceous ornamentals.*

Black cohosh (Cimicifuga racemosa, *at left*) *and Virginia bluebells* (Mertensia virginica, *above*) *are among the native plants grown in the gardens of Monticello and included among the collections of the Center for Historic Plants. The French, or stick-a-dove, lavender* (Lavandula stoechas, *at right*) *was grown in Virginia gardens as early as 1735.*

155

Wine at Monticello

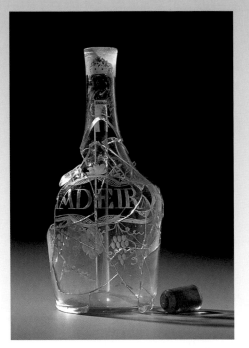

THOMAS JEFFERSON'S KNOWLEDGEABLE AND ENDURING FASCINATION WITH WINE and his pioneering experiments in grape growing at Monticello have endowed him with the reputation as America's "first distinguished viticulturist." Jefferson advised George Washington, John Adams, James Monroe, and James Madison on suitable wines for the White House cellars; kept detailed and often-quoted notes on his wine-tasting travels through Provence, northern Italy, and Germany; and imported extravagant quantities of Europe's most esteemed wines for his own cellars at Monticello and in Washington, where his account books reveal purchases during his eight years of service of over twenty thousand bottles of wine for presidential dinners.

Jefferson served wine after dinner daily, and numerous visitors to both Monticello and the President's House attested to the spirited conversations that ensued, whether about politics or about Jefferson's multifaceted interests in architecture, art, music, or literature. His own vibrant refrains on wine animate the story: when he said, "No nation is drunken where wine is cheap," or, "Wine from long habit has become an indispensable for my health," he provides inspiration for the wine enthusiast and grower alike. Jefferson believed that his native land had the "soil, aspect, and climate of the best wine countries" and that, "We could, in the United States, make as great a variety of wine as are made in Europe, not exactly of the same kinds, but doubtless as good." Perhaps most importantly, Jefferson's curious promotion of American-made wine and his association with other pioneering grape growers stimulated experimental viticulture in the New World.

This labeled Madeira decanter, excavated from the dry well site of the Monticello kitchen yard, dates from the 1760s. English-made, it is decorated with a cartouche and grapevine motifs. After his death, twelve decanters were recorded in an inventory; some of these might have been those that he had shipped back from France in 1790.

(Right) This seau crénelé, *a crenellated vessel for rinsing wine glasses, was part of a service decorated with* guirlande de barbeaux *(cornflower garland) made at the royal French porcelain factory at Sèvres exclusively for the use of Louis XVI at Versailles. How Jefferson obtained this and a* sucrier *(sugar bowl) from the same service is not known.*

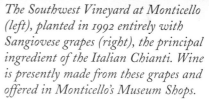

The Southwest Vineyard at Monticello (left), planted in 1992 entirely with Sangiovese grapes (right), the principal ingredient of the Italian Chianti. Wine is presently made from these grapes and offered in Monticello's Museum Shops.

Jefferson owned many styles of stemware purchased between 1767 and 1821, including these English lead-glass examples with a band of wheel-cut sprig and oval engraving. By 1826, only seventeen wine glasses were mentioned in the household inventory made after Jefferson's death.

The Plantation

A Day in the Life

The summer of 1814 was a time of national anxiety. "We are all on the alert as to the fate of Washington," Jefferson wrote to a neighbor on August 27, not yet aware that three days earlier the British army had entered the federal city and set fire to its public buildings.[1] Even in the midst of war, however, life on the Monticello plantation proceeded according to its usual unchanging rhythms, and its seventy-one-year-old proprietor continued to follow his own daily regimen. Although Jefferson's precise actions on any one day can never be fully recovered, his monumental archive provides sufficient information about the activities of August 1814 to evoke a typical plantation day in that month.

After a morning committed to his burdensome correspondence, Jefferson devoted the middle of the day to outdoor activities that satisfied his belief in the importance of daily physical exercise as well as his need to supervise his plantation operations. He first walked along Mulberry Row, the hub of plantation activity, to monitor the work of his tradesmen. Joseph Fossett and Moses Hern were in the blacksmith shop, attaching an iron moldboard—made to Jefferson's own innovative design—to a large wooden plow. They had been unable to make nails since they used the last supply of nailrod, shipped before the British blockaded the Chesapeake ports. In the joinery, John Hemings awaited

by Lucia Stanton, Shannon Senior Research Historian at Monticello

Nails, nailrod, and nail-making tools excavated on Mulberry Row recall an industry that was pursued by enslaved men and boys at Monticello for thirty years.

Jefferson's orders for a set of bookshelves. His brother Peter Hemings was preparing equipment in the malthouse for the autumn brewing of beer.

Jefferson stopped at the textile shop, normally the domain of his daughter Martha Randolph. When he passed the stone building now known as the Weaver's Cottage, he thought he would ask fourteen-year-old Israel Gillette, who was both a groom and a carder in the shop, to return to the stable to saddle his horse.

Gillette and three other boys prepared the fiber for the spinners, five women and teenaged girls who operated machines with twenty-four to forty-eight spindles. The spinners produced yarn of wool, cotton, and hemp that was woven into cloth by Mary Hern and Dolly on looms with flying shuttles.

After Jefferson mounted his bay horse Bremo, he rode down the mountain through pastures where a flock of Barbary broadtail sheep was tended by a young shepherd, aided by a French sheepdog. A mile from the mountaintop, Jefferson reached the Monticello farm quarters, where he and overseer Edmund Bacon discussed the prospects for the corn crop.

Continuing down the mountain to the Rivanna River, Jefferson entered the River Field, in which foreman James Hern and several other men and women were clearing the field of briars and stones before the October planting of wheat. Jefferson paused at his new sawmill at the edge of the field, where head carpenter Roland Goodman was supervising three men repairing the waterwheel that drove the mill, and pondered a solution to the problem of insufficient water from the sawmill canal.

Jefferson's Mulberry Row stable housed his fine blooded carriage and saddle horses, while the stalls under the North Terrace (shown here as restored in 1938) accommodated the horses of Monticello visitors.

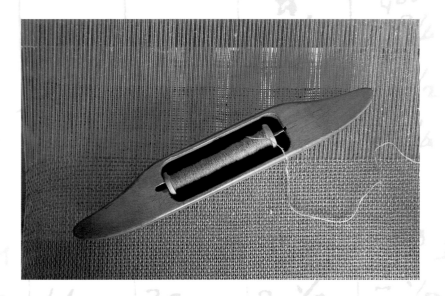

This stone structure on Mulberry Row (much altered since Jefferson's time) once housed a textile shop where enslaved women and children turned cotton, hemp, and wool into cloth for the laborers. Archaeological excavations along Mulberry Row unearthed evidence of women's occupations after their day's labor was done, including needles, pins, and thimbles, and pieces of cow bone, from which they punched out buttons.

Jefferson's chart of the daily tasks of his textile workers indicates that their workday lengthened with the sunlight, from nine hours in midwinter to fourteen hours in midsummer.

(Following pages) Artist G. B. McIntosh illustrated the multiple activities on Mulberry Row, which was lined with wood- and ironworking shops, storehouses for iron and charcoal, structures for domestic occupations, and six dwellings for free and enslaved workers. This detail shows slave dwellings, the textile shop in a former dwelling, the wash house, the dairy and smokehouse, and the nailery-blacksmith shop.

Jefferson's manufacturing mill, completed in 1807, processed local wheat into flour, which was then shipped down the Rivanna River to market in Richmond. Jefferson leased out this mill, here illustrated in a magazine from 1853.

(Opposite) View from Monticello in early morning.

Low water in the Rivanna River made fording easy. Jefferson crossed over to the Lego farm, where overseer Elijah Ham was directing a group of laborers cutting clover in the Triangle Field. Ham reported that the threshing machine, which had processed over 150 bushels of the summer's wheat crop the day before, needed repair. Jefferson proceeded downstream, along a canal beside the river to the Shadwell farm. On the opposite bank, on the Tufton farm, he could see David Hern carefully stacking split sticks of wood to make a dome-shaped kiln, which he would cover with turf and set alight. This kiln would produce 974 bushels of charcoal, fuel for the forges of the blacksmiths and some of the stoves in the house.

Jefferson had now reached the bustling site of his millworks at Shadwell, where two mills filled the air with the crashing sounds of gears and machinery. He passed a mule cart, driven by Jerry, loaded with cornmeal for the main house. At the toll mill, which ground grain for home use, he agreed to buy a dozen Guinea fowl from miller Ewen Carden. Jefferson had leased out the larger mill, which ground his and his neighbors' market wheat. This merchant mill had two pairs of millstones and the most up-to-date milling machinery, patented by Oliver Evans. Its tenants purchased their flour barrels from Jefferson's coopers' shops, where he dismounted to talk to Barnaby Gillette and Nace about the need for increasing production from four to six barrels a day. The market flour was shipped down the Rivanna and James rivers to Richmond. Jefferson's flour from the 1813 wheat crop was still there; as he wrote this month, because of the war, "none can be sold at any price."

Jefferson rode farther downstream before crossing back to the south side of the Rivanna and the small town of Milton, more than three miles from where he had begun on Mulberry Row. After stopping to negotiate a contract with a man who wished to cut

Monticello as seen from Montalto, the mountain that rises above Monticello to the southwest. About sixty African Americans lived on or near the top of Monticello Mountain.

firewood on his lands surrounding the town, he ended his outward journey on the slopes behind Milton with a bit of quail shooting. In his daily combination of exercise and plantation management, Jefferson probably rode as much as ten miles, never leaving his own property.

The Land

In August 1814, Jefferson's Albemarle County plantation contained 5,375 acres on both sides of the Rivanna River. At the Monticello home farm and two quarter farms, Tufton and Lego, almost a thousand acres were under cultivation. Jefferson had given the Shadwell farm to his grandson, and he did not grow crops on Montalto, the mountain rising above Monticello to the southwest; its forest cover provided a source of hardwood and woodland grazing for pigs and cattle.

Jefferson had inherited three thousand acres from his father, Peter Jefferson, in 1764. For almost thirty years afterward, he followed the usual course of Virginia plantation owners. With the labor of slaves, he raised tobacco as his main cash crop, which he sold to a Scottish mercantile firm, and grew Indian corn to feed his laborers and livestock. In his *Notes on the State of Virginia*, he condemned this mode of agriculture, writing that the cultivation of tobacco was "productive of infinite wretchedness." Raising a tobacco crop and getting it to market required exhausting labor over eighteen months: planting, transplanting, weeding, topping, suckering, deworming, cutting, curing, stripping, stemming, and finally, prizing into hogsheads to be shipped to inspection warehouses. "The men and animals on these farms are badly fed," Jefferson observed, "and the earth is rapidly impoverished."[2]

Nevertheless, it was not until the early 1790s that Jefferson began to transform Monticello from a tobacco plantation to a wheat farm. He banished tobacco from his

(Following pages) View from Montalto, including part of Jefferson's Tufton quarter farm, a mile from the Monticello house. Tufton provided some of his best agricultural land. Besides its annual crop of wheat, Tufton was the source of much of the corn, oats, hay, pork, beef, lamb, and butter for the support of the Monticello house and plantation. From 1817, Jefferson's grandson Thomas Jefferson Randolph leased and lived at Tufton.

Jefferson received a gold medal from a French agricultural society for his improved moldboard for a plow, now considered his one true invention. He conceived his design for the "moldboard of least resistance" while traveling through eastern France in 1788. Woodworker Robert L. Self and blacksmith Peter Ross used Jefferson's drawings to make this full-scale model of a barshare plow with a Jeffersonian moldboard.

his fellow countrymen. In the 1790s he had refined his design for a "moldboard of least resistance" for a plow, communicating its benefits through letters, diagrams, and models that he sent to both Americans and Europeans. He imported a model of the recently patented Scottish threshing machine, "to save the labours of my countrymen."[7] Hoping his neighbors would profit by his example, he had three machines based on this model erected at Monticello.

The sale of an annual crop of wheat or flour was dependent on events taking place hundreds and often thousands of miles away. The Embargo of 1807, the War of 1812, and, finally, severe agricultural depression after 1818 all adversely affected Jefferson's income from his plantation. "I am not fit to be a farmer with the kind of labour that we have," he wrote in 1799, discouraged by the difficulty of managing his enslaved farm laborers so that productivity was achieved without cruelty.[8] His absences in public service defeated his plan for the systematic improvement of his own farms, and he never accommodated his ideal rural vision to the realities of slavery. But Jefferson continued to be the most articulate spokesman for an agrarian ideal of a nation of independent farmers—industrious, virtuous, and self-governing. Agriculture, he wrote in 1821, is "the happiest [employment] we can follow, and the most important to our country."[9]

The Laborers

Jefferson was heir to men, women, and children as well as land. At Monticello he perpetuated the same system of management his father had practiced before him. Enslaved men and women cultivated the crops; cared for the livestock; drove the carts and wagons; built and maintained the fences, farm buildings, and machinery; and made thousands of yards of cloth. Their activities were supervised by overseers, mostly local men hired by the year.

From his father's estate, Jefferson had inherited about twenty people, who by 1774 had, through the birth of children, increased to forty-seven. In that year, a further 135 enslaved African Americans became his property after the division of the estate of his father-in-law, John Wayles. Thereafter, Jefferson owned in any one year around two hundred slaves, about two-thirds of them residents on the Monticello plantation while the rest lived at Poplar Forest in Bedford County.

Nathaniel Gibbs's painting Cornstalks *illustrates one of the labor-intensive crops of the Monticello plantation. Indian corn provided the staple food of the enslaved men and women, who received a peck of cornmeal each week.*

*The stone chimney of the joinery
stands as a solitary reminder of the
bustling activity on Mulberry Row
in the years of Jefferson's residence.
It is one of only three structures
remaining, in part, of the seventeen
original buildings that once lined
Monticello's busiest thoroughfare.
Joiners like John Hemings, a slave,
and James Dinsmore, a free workman,
here fashioned mahogany furniture
and the decorative woodwork for
the main house.*

By 1814, there were almost 175 people living on the Monticello plantation: on the home farm, at Tufton on the south side of the Rivanna River, and at Lego on the north side. Besides Jefferson's own family, this total included three overseers, the head carpenter, the miller, their families, and 135 enslaved African-American men, women, and children. At the farms, the workers were in the fields from dawn to dusk, six days a week, while the older women cared for the young children and did the cooking. The farm laborers worked, according to the Monticello custom, in "gangs" of half men, half women, and both men and women drove the plows.

About sixty African Americans lived on or near the top of Monticello Mountain, along Mulberry Row, or in scattered locations on its slopes. They were the house servants, the blacksmiths and carpenters, grooms and gardeners, the carters and wagoners, and the textile workers. Mulberry Row was the hub of plantation activities, with its iron- and wood-working shops, the weaving room, and dwellings for free and enslaved workers.

Lucy Cottrell, who was probably born at Monticello, holds Charlotte Elizabeth Blatterman about 1850. Lucy's mother, Dorothea (Dolly) Cottrell, was an enslaved domestic servant in the household of Jefferson's daughter Martha J. Randolph and thus lived at Monticello after 1809. Both Dolly and Lucy Cottrell were freed by the Blatterman family of Maysville, Kentucky, in 1855.

The level of skills in those shops was remarkably high. As Jefferson wrote in 1816, "To be independent for the comforts of life, we must fabricate them ourselves."[10] Monticello's location far from the markets of large towns or cities required a significant degree of self-sufficiency. Especially during the periods of construction on the main house, Jefferson brought to the mountaintop artisans with a wide array of skills, free men recently arrived from Ireland, Scotland, and Germany, as well as Americans. The black-

The couple illustrated in In the Vegetable Garden *by Nathaniel Gibbs can represent Bagwell and Minerva, enslaved farm laborers at Monticello. Records reveal that after their long days working in the wheat and tobacco fields, they tended their own garden, selling to Jefferson cucumbers, squash, watermelons, and a large crop of hops.*

smith William Stewart, weaver William Maclure, carpenters James Dinsmore and John Neilson, and stonecutter John Gorman practiced their trades at Monticello and trained enslaved men and women, who in turn passed these skills on to other members of their families and community.

Jefferson's free overseers and workmen were paid annual wages between $100 and $275 and given allowances of bacon and cornmeal as well as housing. The enslaved men and women were unpaid, except for occasional "premiums" for the coopers, charcoalburners, and blacksmiths as an incentive to increase productivity. The weekly food rations for each adult consisted of a peck of cornmeal, a half-pound of pork or pickled beef, and four salted fish. Their annual cloth distributions included both a summer and winter suit of clothes, plus a blanket every three years and occasional hats, socks, and shoes. Evidently no furnishings, except for certain cooking utensils, were provided for their cabins.

It is evident that, in their free time, many of Monticello's enslaved men and women continued to work in order to supplement their allotments of food, clothing, and furnishings. In the evenings and on Sunday, they tended their gardens and poultry yards, raising extra vegetables and chickens to sell to their master; they fished and hunted to vary their diet; they made furniture and clothing for their own households and items like brooms and wooden pails to sell; they also performed tasks outside their working hours for which Jefferson paid them.

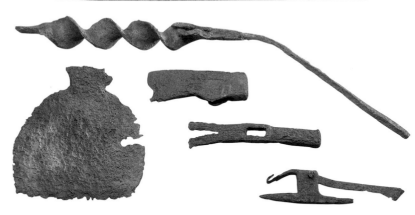

In 1774 Jefferson inherited 135 slaves, in addition to the 52 he already owned, from his father-in-law, John Wayles. He then inaugurated what he called his Farm Book by making a list of the enslaved men, women, and children at Monticello and his other plantations in Virginia.

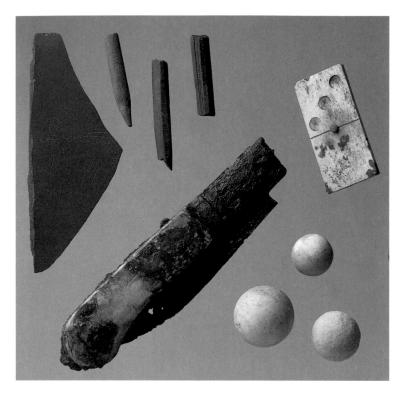

(Above) Artifacts excavated along Mulberry Row, including a piece of slate with the fragmentary words of a writing lesson on it, recall the leisure time activities of the slaves.

(Opposite) Nathaniel Gibbs's A Story Told captures the spirit of nighttime in the Monticello slave quarters, when the workday was over. The records suggest that a rich cultural life, full of storytelling, music and dancing, visiting, and prayer meetings, found expression after sunset.

In the intervals of after-hours labor to earn money, care for their families, and improve their living conditions, the enslaved men and women activated a web of connections that bound them together into a community. Sunday was a time for visiting among the quarter farms of the plantation or beyond its borders, for which written permission from master or overseer was usually required. Nights and Sundays were also full of music and dancing, sports, religious observances, and the occasional midnight excursion in search of possum or wild honey. A number of Jefferson's slaves were eager to read and write, and they sought an education from their relatives or from members of Jefferson's family. As one former Monticello slave recalled, "I learned to read by inducing the white children to teach me the letters."[11]

Documentary records and oral history reveal strong family and community ties in the dwellings of Monticello's African Americans, where skills and values were passed from generation to generation. David and Isabel Hern had fifty-five children and grandchildren who lived in bondage at Monticello. Hern was a skilled woodworker and wheelwright, and his wife was a domestic servant. Of their sons, James was a foreman of labor, Moses a blacksmith, David a wagoner, and Thrimston a carpenter and stonecutter. Their daughter Lily was a farm laborer, while Edith Hern learned French cookery at the President's House and was head cook at Monticello for many years.

Over forty members of another family lived at Monticello. Edward and Jane Gillette, whose marriage linked the Jefferson and Wayles populations, were both farm workers. Their daughters Fanny and Susan were, respectively, a cook and a nursemaid.

The worlds of the house and plantation
converged in the Monticello kitchen.
In 1814, the vegetables grown by head
gardener Wormley Hughes and meat
raised by foreman James Hern were
transformed into meals for Jefferson and
his family by enslaved women and boys.
The head cooks were Edith Fossett and
Fanny Hern; Israel Gillette and Robert
Colbert worked under them as scullions.

Peter Hemings was the first resident of
the cook's room (above) adjacent to the
kitchen. He had become head cook on the
departure, in 1796, of his freed brother
James, who penned this inventory of the
Monticello kitchen (at right). In 1809 one
of the two cooks trained in French cookery
in the President's House in Washington,
Edith Fossett or Fanny Hern, moved
into this space.

Isaac Jefferson, born in slavery at Monticello in 1775, worked as a nail maker and blacksmith. He also briefly operated a Mulberry Row tin shop, following several years spent learning tinsmithing in Philadelphia. After gaining his freedom in the 1820s, he moved to Petersburg, Virginia, where he was photographed, still practicing his blacksmithing trade, at the age of seventy-two.

Their son Barnaby was a cooper, and his younger brothers Gill, James, and Israel worked in the Monticello house and kitchen and drove Jefferson's carriage. The recollections of Israel Gillette, who took the surname Jefferson in freedom, were published in 1873.

One family that Jefferson purchased in 1773 held positions of great importance. George was a foreman of labor who rose to occupy the post of overseer, the only enslaved man to do so. His wife Ursula was a pastry cook and laundress who directed many of the domestic operations at Monticello. Their son George managed the Mulberry Row nailery, while Bagwell was a farm laborer and Isaac a tinsmith and blacksmith. In 1847, Isaac, who used the surname Jefferson in freedom, left his recollections of life at Monticello.

*Charcoal and pit coal fueled the
forges of Monticello's blacksmiths
and nail makers. In its prime, the
Mulberry Row nailery produced
eight to ten thousand nails a day.*

Mulberry Row's road surface, its namesake trees, and part of the paling fence surrounding the vegetable garden and orchard have been restored. The buildings that lined it are the major missing elements. In 1796 this view would have included a washhouse, a smokehouse-dairy, and a storehouse for iron.

Despite lifelong efforts to make his operations more efficient and productive, as well as imaginative enterprises like the nailery and millworks, Jefferson seldom made a profit from his plantation. His long career in public service prevented full attention to his personal affairs, while international wars and national crises affected the market price of his staple crops. Finally, severe agricultural depression after 1818 accelerated a deepening cycle of debt. Jefferson died in 1826 owing over $100,000. His furnishings, books and paintings, farm equipment, and finally his house and lands were sold off to help pay the immense debt.

EXECUTOR'S SALE.

Will be sold, on the fifteenth of January, at Monticello, in the county of Albemarle, the whole of the residue of the personal estate of Thomas Jefferson, dec., consisting of **130 VALUABLE NEGROES,** Stock, Crop, &c. Household and Kitchen Furniture. The attention of the public is earnestly invited to this property. The negroes are believed to be the most valuable for their number ever offered at one time in the State of Virginia. The household furniture, many valuable historical and portrait paintings, busts of marble and plaister of distinguished individuals; one of marble of Thomas Jefferson, by Caracci, with its pedestal and truncated column on which it stands; a polygraph or copying instrument used by Thomas Jefferson, for the last twenty-five years; with various other articles curious and useful to men of business and private families. The terms of sale will be accommodating and made known previous to the day. The sale will be continued from day to day until completed. The sale being unavoidable, it is a sufficient guarantee to the public, that it will take place at the time and place appointed.

THOMAS J. RANDOLPH,
Executor of Th: Jefferson, dec.
January 6, 1827—2t

Jefferson freed only seven enslaved men in his lifetime or in his will; four other slaves were allowed to run away without pursuit. He had often expressed concern for improving the living conditions of his own slaves. The food, clothing, and housing he provided, although inadequate by twentieth-century standards, were considered better than the southern standard. He also tried, with some success, to reduce the use of excessive physical punishment. Having, as he said, "scruples about selling negroes but for delinquency, or on their own request," Jefferson only reluctantly bought or sold slaves.[12] Economic difficulties, however, forced him to sell over 120 slaves during his lifetime, and his death left the remainder unprotected from sale and separation.

Men, women, and children accounted for 90 percent of the value of Jefferson's estate at his death. In 1827 and 1829, 130 people were sold at auction, dispersing a community that had occupied Monticello for as long as Jefferson himself.

Because Jefferson died leaving debts totaling over $100,000, his household furniture, books and paintings, farm equipment, and eventually house and land were sold in the five years after his death. The 130 men, women, and children living in slavery at Monticello accounted for 90 percent of the appraised value of his estate. Monticello's African-American families were dispersed by sale in 1827 and 1829.

Henry Martin, who for many years rang the bell in the Rotunda of the University of Virginia, recalled that he was born at Monticello on the day Jefferson died. His enslaved parents worked in the Monticello house.

(Following pages) The south dependencies, completed in 1808, included a dairy, a smokehouse, three rooms for enslaved house servants, and the kitchen.

The Hemings Family

FIVE GENERATIONS OF THE FAMILY OF Elizabeth (Betty) Hemings—more than eighty people—lived and worked at Monticello, occupying some of the most important domestic and artisans' positions there. Her daughters Bett, Critta, and Sally worked in the house, and Nance was a skilled weaver. Betty's son Robert was Jefferson's personal servant, and Robert's brother Martin and nephew Burwell Colbert were butlers. Both James and Peter Hemings were cooks, the former trained in Paris; the youngest of Betty Hemings's sons, John, was a highly skilled cabinetmaker and joiner who helped fabricate Monticello's decorative interior woodwork and made many articles of furniture.

This small bell was preserved by the descendants of Betty Hemings as a gift from Jefferson's dying wife, Martha, to their ancestor. The French ointment pot (left), found in excavations below Mulberry Row, may have been brought back from Paris by James or Sally Hemings.

The Hemings family had a unique access to freedom. All seven slaves freed by Jefferson in his lifetime and in his will were Betty Hemings's sons or grandsons, and her daughter Sally was the only African American at Monticello whose children were able to live their entire adult lives in freedom. Her sons Madison and Eston Hemings, carpenters who learned their trade from their uncle John, received their freedom in Jefferson's will in 1826. Their siblings Beverly and Harriet Hemings had been allowed to leave Monticello some years earlier, when they were twenty-one. In 1873 Madison Hemings spoke about his life at Monticello, confirming his belief that he and his siblings were the children of Thomas Jefferson. This connection was privately denied by Jefferson's daughter Martha Randolph and her family, and the issue has been part of American public discourse for two centuries. Because of genetic testing in 1998 and an ensuing review of other kinds of evidence, most historians today accept the truth of Madison Hemings's statement and believe that he and his siblings were Thomas Jefferson's children.

Elizabeth-Ann Isaacs and her brother Peter Fossett were Betty Hemings's great-grandchildren, born in slavery at Monticello to Joseph and Edith Fossett, the head blacksmith and head cook. Peter Fossett became, in freedom, a prominent Baptist minister in Ohio.

This indenture witnesseth that I Thomas Jefferson of the
county of Albemarle have manumitted and made free
Robert Hemings, son of Betty Hemings: so that in future
he shall be free & of free condition, with all his goods & chattels
and shall be discharged of all obligation of bondage or servitude
whatsoever: and that neither myself, my heirs executors or admini-
-strators shall have any right to exact from him hereafter
services or duties whatsoever. in witness whereof I have put
seal to this present deed of manumission. Given in Albem
this twenty fourth day of December one thousand
and ninety four.

Signed, sealed and
delivered in presence of
D. Carr.

Th. Jefferson

Jefferson granted freedom to seven
men, all Betty Hemings's sons or
grandsons. The first was Robert
Hemings, freed by this Christmas
Eve deed. John Hemings and his
nephew Madison Hemings registered
as free men (below) several years
after Jefferson's will gave them
their freedom.

Many members of the Hemings
family passed back and forth along
this underground passageway, which
linked the domestic activities of the
kitchen, smokehouse, washhouse,
and storerooms with the main house.
The bells of Monticello's interior
bell system rang in this passage to
summon waiters, maids, or butler
Burwell Colbert.

Robert Hughes, another great-
grandchild of Betty Hemings, was
born at Monticello in 1824, the son
of head gardener Wormley Hughes
and his wife, Ursula. Robert Hughes
became the founding minister of
Union Run Baptist Church east
of Charlottesville.

Mulberry Row

THE CENTER OF PLANTATION OPERATIONS AT MONTICELLO WAS A ONE-thousand-foot-long road Jefferson called Mulberry Row, after the trees that lined it. At the height of activity in 1796, there were seventeen structures along Mulberry Row, from the stable at its northeast end to the sheds for storing charcoal to the southwest. In between were five log dwellings for slaves, a stone house for free resident workmen, a wash house, a smokehouse and dairy, a blacksmith shop and nailery, two woodworking shops, and buildings for storage.

Since most of these structures were built of wood, little survives from Jefferson's time. The stone workmen's house, altered over the years, today contains offices. Only portions of two other buildings remain—the stone stable, once home to Jefferson's saddle and carriage horses, and the stone chimney of the joinery, where much of the fine architectural woodwork for the house was crafted.

With its woodworking and ironworking shops and its textile operations, Mulberry Row made Monticello a kind of industrial village, independent and self-sustaining. The enslaved artisans, often trained by hired white craftsmen, achieved a high level of expertise in a variety of trades.

In 1808 Jefferson had his log stable, at the northeast end of Mulberry Row, rebuilt in stone. Here Wormley Hughes looked after Jefferson's carriage and saddle horses Bremo, Diomede, Tecumseh, Wellington, and Eagle.

In 1981 archaeologists uncovered the remains of one of the slave dwellings on Mulberry Row, revealing its stone foundation, earth floor, brick-lined root cellars, and many discarded artifacts.

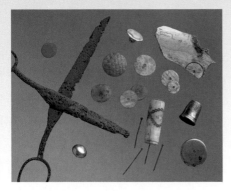

These reminders of the sewing activities of Monticello's enslaved African Americans are among the artifacts unearthed on Mulberry Row. Women mended and embellished their family's clothing at night, and tailor Peter Hemings spent his days making shirts and trousers for the enslaved men.

In A Moment on Mulberry Row, *artist Nathaniel Gibbs sought to depict the lives of Monticello's African Americans in the hours when they were not working in the fields and shops. His images evoke activities like fishing and raising poultry that characterized the efforts of enslaved families to improve their living conditions.*

Jefferson's early sketch plan for multi-family housing for slaves was probably not built in this form. In 1796 there were five single-family log dwellings (the boxes r, s, t, q, and o on his plat) on Mulberry Row, ranging in size from twelve by fourteen feet to fourteen by seventeen feet.

TRADES AND
Technology

ECONOMY AND EFFICIENCY WERE TWO MAJOR GOALS OF JEFFERSON'S PLANTATION operations. He had his enslaved laborers trained in a wide variety of skills, experimented with the most up-to-date labor-saving machinery, and inaugurated several enterprises to provide income to supplement the sales of annual crops of wheat or tobacco. In a nail-making shop, enslaved boys aged ten to twenty began to produce eight to ten thousand nails a day in 1794. The War of 1812, and the Embargo that preceded it, prompted Jefferson to expand his textile operations to provide the cloth needed for Monticello's enslaved families. From 1813 women and girls in the mechanized textile shop at Mulberry Row made two thousand yards of cloth a year. Jefferson hoped that the mill he had built on the Rivanna River at his Shadwell farm would provide a reliable source of income by grinding the area's market wheat. A smaller grist mill processed wheat and corn for home consumption, receiving a percentage of the flour and cornmeal in toll.

Jefferson was one of the first in his county to use the newly patented Scottish threshing machine for his wheat crop, and in the 1790s he developed his "moldboard of least resistance," an improved moldboard for a plow. He did not patent his invention, "having never thought of monopolizing by patent any useful idea which happens to offer itself to me."

Jefferson designed his "moldboard of least resistance" (shown on this small scale model of a barshare plow) on mathematical principles to turn the cut sod over with the least expenditure of force.

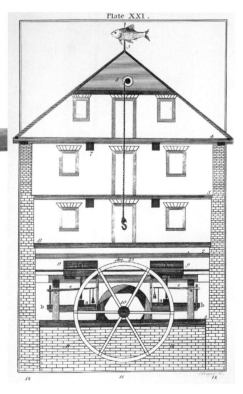

Jefferson's large manufacturing mill was similar to this one, with two pairs of millstones and the latest milling machinery patented by Oliver Evans.

G. B. McIntosh's illustration of building trades at Monticello shows a turning lathe and the hand sawing of plank. In 1813, Jefferson began construction of a complex millworks which used the Rivanna River to operate a sawmill, threshing machine, hemp break, hominy beater, winnowers, and a pair of millstones to grind corn and plaster of Paris.

The cup excavated on Mulberry Row was probably made by Isaac Jefferson, enslaved tinsmith and blacksmith.

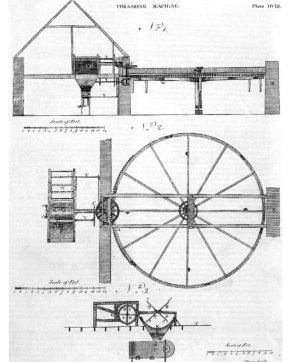

In order "to save the labours of my countrymen," Jefferson imported a model of this drum-and-beater threshing machine from England. He had three machines built for Monticello, driven by horses and by water.

When he was at Monticello, Jefferson monitored the activities of his nailery daily, weighing the iron and nails to calculate the productivity and efficiency of the young workers. They hammered six sizes of nails by hand and used a machine to cut four-penny brads.

The War of 1812 stimulated textile production all across the United States. By 1815 the textile shop on Mulberry Row had three Hargreaves spinning jennies (shown here) with twenty-four spindles each, looms with fly shuttles, and a carding machine. There thirteen enslaved women and children turned cotton, wool, and hemp into cloth.

195

Archaeology

AT MONTICELLO

ARCHAEOLOGICAL RESEARCH PLAYS AN IMPORTANT ROLE in the attempt to recover a more complete picture of the complex social and economic community that flourished at Monticello during Thomas Jefferson's lifetime. Monticello's archaeologists have investigated the below-ground traces of the plantation outbuildings that once stood along Mulberry Row and the orchards and Vegetable Garden to the south of it. During this work, thousands of artifacts were recovered, along with the remains of vanished buildings, fences, and other landscape features.

Archaeological research at Monticello is reaching beyond the confines of the mountaintop with the first systematic archaeological survey of the two thousand acres of land that formed the core of Jefferson's five-thousand-acre plantation. Among the key findings thus far is the location of at least one slave burial ground on the property. Another emphasis of Monticello's present archaeological work is re-examining our long-held assumptions about Mulberry Row, a reminder that understanding our history is an ongoing, changing process.

—Fraser Neiman, *Director of Archaeology at Monticello*

An ebony ring and cowrie shell hint at the persistence of African materials and usages at Monticello. In seventeenth and eighteenth-century West Africa, cowries had monetary and symbolic value, and were used for personal adornment, hung on a string, or sewn to clothing. Pierced European and American coins represent an African-American reinvention of the tradition. They also document slaves' access to cash and participation in the regional economy.

Fashionable ceramics, like the Chinese porcelain pictured here, are common on slave domestic sites at Monticello and elsewhere. Research suggests that much of this material was purchased by enslaved people, and not given to them by their owners. Variation in ceramic styles among sites hints at both an interest among some slaves in stylish ceramics and varying amounts expended to acquire them.

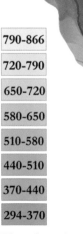

| 790-866 |
| 720-790 |
| 650-720 |
| 580-650 |
| 510-580 |
| 440-510 |
| 370-440 |
| 294-370 |

Elevation (feet)

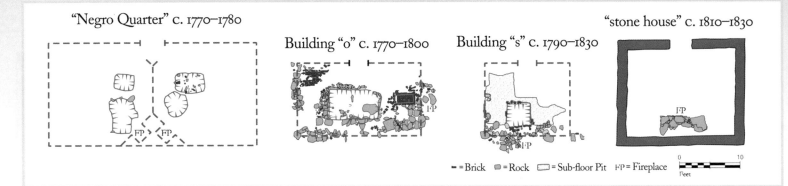

"Negro Quarter" c. 1770–1780

Building "o" c. 1770–1800

Building "s" c. 1790–1830

"stone house" c. 1810–1830

▪ = Brick ◼ = Rock ▭ = Sub-floor Pit FP = Fireplace

0   10
Feet

Housing for enslaved people was a prominent feature of the Monticello mountaintop landscape from 1769 to 1826. On Mulberry Row, most slaves lived in clay-chinked log cabins with dirt floors, clay-lined wood chimneys, and unmortared stone foundations. The plans of the buildings changed significantly over time. Archaeology reveals that slave houses built in the 1770s and 1780s had larger rooms, about 260 square feet, and two sub-floor pits under each room (see "Negro Quarter" and Building "o"). After 1790,

room sizes declined to about 160 square feet. While a few rooms had a single, small sub-floor pit, most rooms lacked them entirely (Building "s"). The shift probably represents an increase in the influence some slaves had over their housing situations, and their preference to live in smaller, family-based groups. Two single-room slave houses built of stone around 1810 had larger rooms and lacked sub-floor pits, indicating that the amount of space allotted to the families who lived in them increased ("stone house").

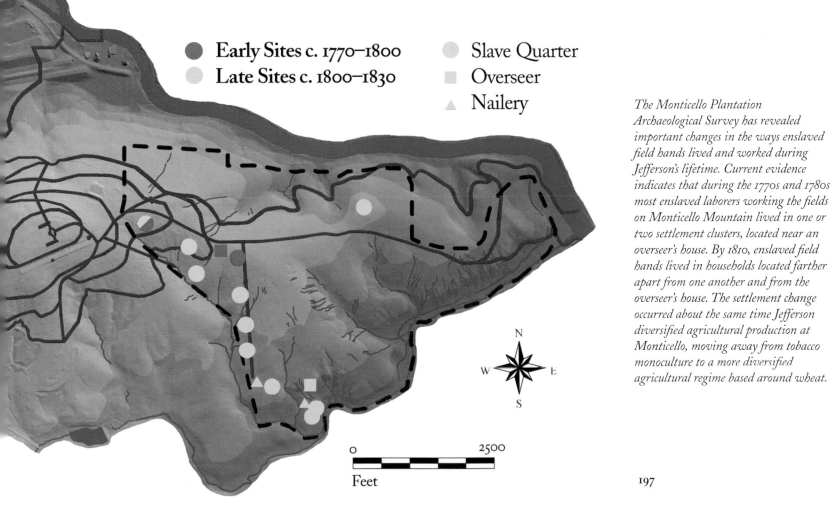

● **Early Sites c. 1770–1800**

● **Late Sites c. 1800–1830**

○ Slave Quarter

■ Overseer

▲ Nailery

The Monticello Plantation Archaeological Survey has revealed important changes in the ways enslaved field hands lived and worked during Jefferson's lifetime. Current evidence indicates that during the 1770s and 1780s most enslaved laborers working the fields on Monticello Mountain lived in one or two settlement clusters, located near an overseer's house. By 1810, enslaved field hands lived in households located farther apart from one another and from the overseer's house. The settlement change occurred about the same time Jefferson diversified agricultural production at Monticello, moving away from tobacco monoculture to a more diversified agricultural regime based around wheat.

0   2500

Feet

Notes

Short Titles and Abbreviations

DLC   Library of Congress, Washington, D.C.

GB   Betts, Edwin M., ed., *Thomas Jefferson's Garden Book*. Philadelphia: The American Philosophical Society, 1944. Reprint, Charlottesville: Thomas Jefferson Memorial Foundation, Inc., 1999.

MB   Bear, James A., Jr., and Lucia C. Stanton, eds., *Jefferson's Memorandum Books: Accounts, with Legal Records and Miscellany, 1767-1826*. Princeton: Princeton University Press, 1997.

MHi   Massachusetts Historical Society, Boston.

Nichols   Nichols, Frederick D., *Thomas Jefferson's Architectural Drawings*, 5th ed. Charlottesville: Thomas Jefferson Memorial Foundation, Inc., 1984.

Papers   Boyd, Julian P., et al., eds., *The Papers of Thomas Jefferson*. 29 vols. to date. Princeton: Princeton University Press, 1950–.

Randall   Randall, Henry S., *The Life of Thomas Jefferson*. New York: Derby and Jackson, 1858.

Smith   Smith, Margaret Bayard, *The First Forty Years of Washington Society*. Edited by Gaillard Hunt. New York: Charles Scribner's Sons, 1906. Reprint, New York: Frederick Ungar Publishing Co., 1965.

ViU   Special Collections, Alderman Library, University of Virginia, Charlottesville.

Visitors   Peterson, Merrill D., ed., *Visitors to Monticello*. Charlottesville: University Press of Virginia, 1989.

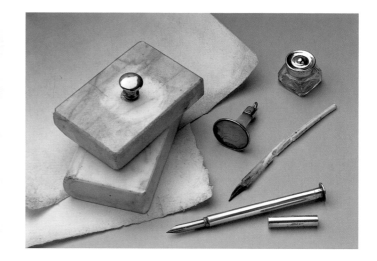

Thomas Jefferson's Essay in Architecture

(pp. 1-39)

[1] TJ to Elbridge Gerry, Philadelphia, 13 May 1797, *The Writings of Thomas Jefferson*, ed. Albert Ellery Bergh (Washington, D.C.: Thomas Jefferson Memorial Association, 1903), 9:381. A version of this essay appeared as "Thomas Jefferson and the Art of Living Out of Doors," in *The Magazine Antiques*, April 2000, 594-605.

[2] TJ to a Reverend Hatch, Monticello, 12 May 1822, Coolidge Collection of Jefferson Manuscripts, MHi.

[3] "Charlottesville-Monticello-Mr. Jefferson-University of VA., From the Letters from a Valetudinarian," *Niles National Register*, 6 July 1839, 301.

[4] TJ to Benjamin Henry Latrobe, Monticello, 10 October 1809, *Correspondence and Miscellaneous Papers of Benjamin Henry Latrobe*, ed. John C. Van Horne and Lee W. Formwalt (New Haven: Yale University Press, for the Maryland Historical Society, Baltimore, 1984-1988), 2:777.

[5] *MB*, 1:76.

[6] The most comprehensive checklist of the drawings is found in Frederick D. Nichols, *Thomas Jefferson's Architectural Drawings*, 5th ed. Many of the drawings were reproduced in Fiske Kimball, *Thomas Jefferson Architect* (Boston: privately published, 1916; reprint, New York: DaCapo Press, 1968).

[7] Jefferson cites Palladio as early as 1769, with entries dating from 1769 in his 1767 Memorandum Book. At the time he owned an English translation of Palladio's *I Quattro Libri del' Architettura* by Giacomo Leoni: *The architecture of A. Palladio* (London, 1742).

For this and other editions of Palladio's works owned by Jefferson, see E. Millicent Sowerby, *Catalogue of the Library of Thomas Jefferson*, 5 vols. (Charlottesville: University Press of Virginia, 1983) and William B. O'Neal, *Jefferson's Fine Arts Library* (Charlottesville: University Press of Virginia, 1976).

8 Marquis de Chastellux, *Travels in North America in the Years 1780, 1781, and 1782*, trans. Howard C. Rice, Jr. (Chapel Hill: University of North Carolina Press, 1963). Quoted in *Visitors*, 12.

9 Ibid.

10 TJ to George Wythe, 23 October 1794, DLC.

11 For a description of the Hôtel de Langeac, the townhouse that Jefferson rented in Paris, see Howard C. Rice, Jr., *Thomas Jefferson's Paris* (Princeton: Princeton University Press, 1976), 51-54.

12 Cited in Jefferson's notebook for the remodeling of the house. See Nichols, nos. 139, pp. 2-4; 145, p. 14; 146, p. 16.

13 See Jefferson's building notebook, Nichols, no. 140, p. 7 and nos. 147-b, pp. 5, 6.

14 TJ to John Brown, 5 April 1797, DLC.

15 Ibid.

16 Jefferson identifies the nursery in his notebook for the remodeling of the house: Nichols, nos. 139, p. 4; 144, p 11; 147-b, pp. 1, 2; 147-c. The Appendix is identified on a floor plan by Jefferson's granddaughter Cornelia Randolph produced shortly after his death; ViU, accession no. 5385-ac, Nichols, no. 563-2. Both are identified in John W. Eppes to TJ, 6 November 1801, MHi.

17 TJ to Mann Page, Monticello, [1796], MHi.

18 TJ to Benjamin Henry Latrobe, Monticello, 8 September 1805, *Correspondence … of Benjamin Henry Latrobe*, 2:140. Blinds were also designed for the large Dining Room skylight.

19 Smith, 72.

20 Ibid., 71.

21 Ellen Randolph Coolidge, quoted in Randall, 3:347.

22 Isaac Weld, *Travels through the States of North America* (London, 1799), quoted in *Visitors*, 19.

23 The location of the workbench is shown on Cornelia Randolph's floor plan; ViU, accession no. 5385-ac, Nichols, no. 563-2. For references to making models see James A. Bear, Jr., ed., *Jefferson at Monticello* (Charlottesville: University Press of Virginia, 1967), p. 84. For references to carpenters' tools and making small things out of metal see p. 18.

24 Nichols, no. 144. On the back of a memorandum (Nichols, no. 147-l verso) dated 24 September 1804 Jefferson included "the Aviary" among the work "reserved" for his slave joiner John Hemings.

25 Smith, 385.

26 TJ to Étienne Lemaire, Monticello, 25 April 1809, MHi.

27 See Nichols, no. 147-p verso; TJ to James Dinsmore, Washington, 28 December 1806, DLC; and TJ to James Dinsmore, Washington, 6 February 1808, MHi.

28 See Nichols, no. 147-m.

29 Ibid., no. 147-q. No. 147-p verso is probably the preliminary study. The Venetian Porches were completed in 2000. Mesick, Cohen, Wilson, Baker, Albany, New York were the architects; fabrication was by Gaston & Wyatt, Charlottesville, Virginia; hardware by The Colonial Williamsburg Foundation and Cersley Masonry. Installation was by Monticello staff members Robert L. Self, Architectural Conservator, and Robert Newcomb, Restoration Specialist, both of whom also constructed the corner terraces. The recreation was based on nineteenth-century photographs (some computer-enhanced); Jefferson's notes and drawings; and physical evidence that confirmed such things as the alignment of the louvered work against the brick walls and the plaster ceiling line. Although green paint was found on the brickwork, it proved to date from the end of the nineteenth century. However, a louvered slat from Jefferson's period was found in the attic with its paint layers intact. The primer is white lead and the first finish coat is verdigris mixed with a small amount of *terre verte* and fillers (probably calcium carbonate). The paint analysis was by Susan Buck, Historic Paint and Architectural Services, Newton Center, Massachusetts. The T. David Fitz-Gibbon Charitable Trust funded the reconstruction of the corner terraces, and the Florence Gould Foundation funded the recreation of the Venetian enclosures.

30 Nichols, nos. 147-p, 147-r.

31 TJ to William Hamilton, Washington, July 1806, DLC.

32 Copy by Ellen Randolph Coolidge of her letter to an unknown recipient, Boston, 27 January [1833 or 1834], Trist Papers, ViU, 6696.

33 Henry Home, Lord Kames, *Elements Of Criticism* (Edinburgh, 1762; reprint, New York: Johnson Reprint, 1967), 3:313. Jefferson knew of this work by 1771 when he recommended it to Robert Skipwith. See TJ to Skipwith, 3 August 1771 in *Papers*, 1:79. For the importance of *Elements Of Criticism* to Jefferson, see the many references in Eleanor D. Berman, *Thomas Jefferson Among the Arts* (New York: Philosophical Library, 1947).

34 For the "angular portals" see Nichols, no. 147-l. Jefferson notes that work on "the 3. remain[in]g Angular Portals" is "reserved for J. Hemings." The fact that three portals are mentioned implies that there were at least four—hence the likelihood that they are at the four corners of the house. The violet bed is identified on Cornelia Randolph's floor plan, Nichols, no. 563-2.

35 Sarah N. Randolph, *The Domestic Life of Thomas Jefferson Compiled from Family Letters and Reminiscences by His Great-Granddaughter* (1871; reprint, Charlottesville: University Press of Virginia, for the Thomas Jefferson Memorial Foundation, 1978), 332. The original terrace roofs and railings were gone by the time of the earliest known photographs of the house. The present restoration dates from 1938-41. The Chinese railings are based on an understanding of Jefferson's intent as well as on several visitors' descriptions and a few early engravings. These views, at best, show a Chinese railing on only a short section of the Northwest Terrace. The patterns used for the restoration are based on railings depicted in early engravings of Jefferson's buildings at the University of Virginia.

36 Bear, *Jefferson at Monticello*, 72.

37 Randall, 3:347.

38 Randolph, *Domestic Life of Thomas Jefferson*, 347.

39 Randall, 3:336.

40 Randolph, *Domestic Life of Thomas Jefferson*, 337.

41 Nichols, no. 147-s.

42 Ibid., nos. 147-l verso and 147-m.

43 Ibid., no. 147-ff verso.

44 Ibid., no. 147-ff verso.

45 Ibid., no . 147-jj.

46 See TJ to James Dinsmore, Washington, 8 June 1805, Herbert R. Strauss Collection, Newberry Library, Chicago.

47 Randall, 3:331.

48 [Margaret Bayard Smith], *Winter in Washington; or, Memoirs of the Seymour Family* (New York: E. Bliss and E. White, 1824), 221. Also in B. L. Rayner, *Sketches of the Life, Writings, and Opinions of Thomas Jefferson* (New York: A. Francis and W. Boardman, 1832), 524.

49 TJ to Benjamin Henry Latrobe, Monticello, 10 October 1809, DLC. Also quoted in *Correspondence … of Benjamin Henry Latrobe*, 2:777. As far as we know Latrobe never visited Monticello.

50 TJ to Martha Jefferson Randolph, Philadelphia, 7 July 1793, DLC.

A Look Inside Monticello

(pp. 40–75)

1 TJ to Angelica Schuyler Church, 27 November 1793, *Papers*, 27:449.

2 Martha Jefferson Randolph to Ellen Randolph Coolidge, 18 September 1825, ViU, 9090.

3 Unidentified daughter to Martha Jefferson Randolph, n.d., ViU, 9090.

4 George Ticknor, 7 February 1815, *Visitors*, 62.

5 Ibid.

6 John French, c. 1825, James A. Bear, compiler, "Descriptions of Monticello, 1780–1826," vol. 1, Research Report, Jefferson Library, Thomas Jefferson Foundation (hereafter, TJF).

7 Randolph, *The Domestic Life of Thomas Jefferson*, 347.

8 George Ticknor, *Life, Letters, and Journals of George Ticknor*, 2 vols. (Boston: James R. Osgood and Company, 1876), 1:36.

9 Virginia Randolph Trist to Ellen Randolph Coolidge, 3 September 1825, ViU, 9090.

10 Martha Jefferson Randolph to Ellen Randolph Coolidge, 2 August 1825, ViU, 9090.

11 Martha Jefferson Randolph to Ellen Randolph Coolidge, 1 September 1825, ViU, 9090.

12 Daniel Webster, *Visitors*, 90.

13 Smith, 69.

14 Ibid., 48.

15 Ticknor, *Life, Letters, and Journals*, 1:36.

16 William Parker Cutler and Julia Perkins Cutler, *Life Journals and Correspondence of Rev. Manasseh Cutler* (Cincinnati, 1888), 2:71-2.

17 Daniel Webster, *Visitors*, 98.

18 Benjamin Henry Latrobe to Mrs. Latrobe, 24 November 1802, *Correspondence … of Benjamin Henry Latrobe*, 1:232.

19 Smith, 67-68.

20 Francis Calley Gray, *Visitors*, 57.

21 Elizabeth Lindsay Gordon cited in Armistead Churchill Gordon, *William Fitzhugh Gordon: A Virginian of the Old School: His Life, Times, and Contemporaries* (NY: Neale, 1909), 58.

22 Cornelia Jefferson Randolph to Ellen Randolph Coolidge, 26 August 1825, ViU, 9090.

23 Ellen Randolph Coolidge to Henry S. Randall, 16 May 1857, ViU, 9090.

24 TJ to N. Burwell, 14 March 1818, cited in Randall, 447.

25 Bear, *Jefferson at Monticello*, 136n.

26 Sir Augustus John Foster, *Visitors*, 39.

27 Sir Augustus John Foster, *Jeffersonian America: Notes on the United States of America Collected in the Years 1805-6-7 and 11-12*, ed. Richard Beale Davis (San Marino, Calif.: Huntington Library, 1954), 144ff.

28 TJ to John Adams, 10 June 1815, in Lester J. Cappon, ed. *The Adams-Jefferson Letters* (Chapel Hill: University of North Carolina Press, 1987), 443.

29 John Edwards Caldwell quoted in William M.E. Rachal, ed., *A Tour through a part of Virginia in the Summer of 1808. (*NY: H C Southwick, 1810; reprint, Richmond: Dietz Press, 1951), 28.

30 Smith, 49-50.

31 Ibid.

32 Ibid., 71.

33 Bear, *Jefferson at Monticello*, 18.

34 Smith, 71.

35 George Tucker, *The Life of Thomas Jefferson, Third President of the United States* (Philadelphia: Carey, Lea & Blanchard, 1837), 190.

36 Daniel Webster, *Visitors*, 98.

37 Virginia Jefferson Randolph to Nicholas P. Trist, 5 June 1823, Nicholas P. Trist Papers, DLC, reel 2/frame 172.

FURNISHING MONTICELLO:
JEFFERSON AS CONSUMER AND COLLECTOR

(pp. 76–111)

1 Howard C. Rice, Jr., *Thomas Jefferson's Paris* (Princeton: Princeton University Press, 1970), 15.

2 *MB*, 1:557.

3 TJ to Samuel Osgood, 5 October 1785, *Papers*, 8:590.

4 For more information on the *marchands merciers,* see Carolyn Sargentson, *Merchants and Luxury Markets: The Marchands Merciers of Eighteenth-Century Paris* (London: Victoria and Albert Museum in association with the J. Paul Getty Museum, 1996).

5 *MB*, 1:565.

6 Ibid.

7 Joseph Spence, *Polymetis: Or An Enquiry concerning the Agreement between the Works of the Roman Poets, and the Remains of the Antient Artists. Being an Attempt to illustrate them mutually from one another.* (1747; reprint, New York: Garland Publishers, 1976), v.

8 TJ to John Trumbull, 30 August 1787, *Papers*, 12:69.

9 TJ to Madame de Bréhan, 19 March 1789, ibid., 14:656.

10 TJ to Madame de Corny, 30 June 1787, ibid., 11:509.

11 TJ to John Page, 4 May 1786, ibid., 9:445.

12 Lucia C. Stanton, in *The Worlds of Thomas Jefferson at Monticello*, ed. Susan R. Stein (New York: Harry N. Abrams, Inc., 1993), 350.

13 TJ to Nathaniel Colley, "Mem. for Capt. Colley to have made in London for Th.J," 16 November 1789, *Papers*, 15:546.

14 TJ to James Madison, 10 January 1791, *Papers*, 18:480.

15 TJ to John Adams, 25 April 1794, in Paul Leicester Ford, ed., *The Writings of Thomas Jefferson*, 12 vols. (New York: G.P. Putnam's Sons, 1904-1905), 6:505.

16 For more information, see Robert L. Self and Susan R. Stein, "The Collaboration of Thomas Jefferson and John Hemings: Furniture Attributed to the Monticello Joinery," *Winterthur Portfolio* 33:4 (Winter 2000): 231-248.

17 TJ to Charles Willson Peale, 6 October 1805, DLC.

18 George Ticknor, *Life, Letters and Journals*, 1:34.

19 TJ to Benjamin Rush, 16 January 1811, in Ford, *Writings*, 11:168.

20 Thomas Jefferson, *Notes on the State of Virginia* (London, 1787; reprint, with notes, William Peden, ed., Chapel Hill: University of North Carolina Press, 1955), 24 (page references are to reprint edition).

Suggested Readings

What follows is a highly selective list. A much more extensive listing "Books on Thomas Jefferson & Monticello," is posted on our web site at http://www.monticello.org, or available free from the Monticello Museum Shop, P.O. Box 316, Charlottesville, Virginia 22902.

On Monticello

William L. Beiswanger, *Monticello in Measured Drawings* (1998)

William M. Kelso, *Archaeology at Monticello* (1997)

Robert C. Lautman, *Thomas Jefferson's Monticello: A Photographic Portrait* (1997)

Jack McLaughlin, *Jefferson and Monticello: The Biography of a Builder* (1988)

Merrill D. Peterson, *Visitors to Monticello* (1989)

Susan R. Stein, *The Worlds of Thomas Jefferson at Monticello* (1993)

Thomas Jefferson Foundation, Inc., *Monticello: A Guidebook* (1997)

Biographical Works

Noble E. Cunningham, Jr., *In Pursuit of Reason: The Life of Thomas Jefferson* (1987)

Dumas Malone, *Jefferson and His Time*, 6 volumes (1948-81)

Dumas Malone, *Thomas Jefferson: A Brief Biography* (1993)

Merrill D. Peterson, *Thomas Jefferson and the New Nation: A Biography* (1970)

Sarah N. Randolph, *The Domestic Life of Thomas Jefferson* (1871; rept. 1985)

Jefferson's Writings

James A. Bear and Lucia C. Stanton, eds, *Jefferson's Memorandum Books*, 2 volumes (1997)

Edwin M. Betts, ed., *Thomas Jefferson's Farm Book* (1953; rept. 1999)

Edwin M. Betts, ed., *Thomas Jefferson's Garden Book* (1944; rept. 1999)

Edwin M. Betts and James A. Bear, Jr., eds, *The Family Letters of Thomas Jefferson* (1966; rept. 1985)

Julian P. Boyd and others, eds., *The Papers of Thomas Jefferson*, 29 volumes (1950-)

Lester J. Cappon, ed., *The Adams-Jefferson Letters* (1959; rept. 1987)

Bernard Mayo, ed., *Jefferson Himself* (1942; rept. 1970)

Merrill D. Peterson, ed., *Thomas Jefferson: Writings* (1984)

Lucia Stanton and Douglas L. Wilson, eds., *Jefferson Abroad* (1999)

On Jefferson's Political Thought and Legacy

Julian P. Boyd and Gerard W. Gawalt, ed., *The Declaration of Independence: The Evolution of the Text* (1999)

Joseph J. Ellis, *American Sphinx: The Character of Thomas Jefferson* (1997)

David N. Mayer, *The Constitutional Thought of Thomas Jefferson* (1994)

Peter S. Onuf, ed., *Jeffersonian Legacies* (1993)

Peter S. Onuf, *Jefferson's Empire* (2000)

Merrill D. Peterson, *The Jefferson Image in the American Mind* (1960)

Robert W. Tucker and David C. Hendrickson, *Empire of Liberty: The Statecraft of Thomas Jefferson* (1990)

Garry Wills, *Inventing America: Jefferson's Declaration of Independence* (1978)

Jefferson's Interests and Special Topics

William Howard Adams, ed., *The Eye of Thomas Jefferson* (1976)

James A. Bear, Jr., ed., *Jefferson at Monticello* (1967)

Silvio A. Bedini, *Jefferson and Science* (2002)

Silvio A. Bedini, *Thomas Jefferson: Statesman of Science* (1990)

Edwin M. Betts and Hazlehurst Bolton Perkins, *Thomas Jefferson's Flower Gardens at Monticello*, 3d edition (1986)

Andrew Burstein, *The Inner Jefferson: Portrait of a Grieving Optimist* (1995)

Andrew Burstein, *Thomas Jefferson: Letters from the Head and Heart* (2002)

Helen C. Cripe, *Thomas Jefferson and Music* (1974)

Noble E. Cunningham, Jr., *Jefferson and Monroe: Constant Friendship and Respect* (2003)

Annette Gordon-Reed, *Thomas Jefferson and Sally Hemings: An American Controversy* (1997)

Peter J. Hatch, *The Fruit and Fruit Trees of Monticello* (1998)

Peter J. Hatch, *The Gardens of Monticello* (1992)

Donald Jackson, *Thomas Jefferson and the Stony Mountains: Exploring the West from Monticello* (1981)

Marc Leepson, *Saving Monticello: The Levy Family's Epic Quest to Rescue the House that Jefferson Built* (2001)

James E. Lewis, Jr., *The Louisiana Purchase: Jefferson's Noble Bargain?* (2003)

Howard C. Rice, *Thomas Jefferson's Paris* (1976)

James P. Ronda, *Jefferson's West: A Journey with Lewis and Clark* (2000)

George Green Shackelford, *Thomas Jefferson's Travels in Europe 1774-1789* (1995)

Eugene R. Sheridan, *Jefferson and Religion* (1998)

Herbert E. Sloan, *Principle and Interest: Thomas Jefferson and the Problem of Debt* (1995)

Lucia Stanton, *Free Some Day: The African-American Families of Monticello* (2000)

Lucia Stanton, *Slavery at Monticello* (1996)

Melvin I. Urofsky, *The Levy Family and Monticello 1834-1923: Saving Thomas Jefferson's House* (2001)

Douglas L. Wilson, *Jefferson's Books* (1996)

Jefferson Bibliography

Frank Shuffelton, *Thomas Jefferson: A Comprehensive Annotated Bibliography of Writings About Him 1826-1980* (1983)

Frank Shuffelton, *Thomas Jefferson, 1981-1990: An Annotated Bibliography* (1992)

Children's Books

Natalie S. Bober, *Thomas Jefferson: Man on a Mountain* (1988)

Ruth Crisman, *Thomas Jefferson: A Man with a Vision* (1992)

Robin H. Gabriel and Dick Ruehrwein, *Discover Jefferson at Monticello* (1989)

Milton Meltzer, *Thomas Jefferson: The Revolutionary Aristocrat* (1991)

Russell Shorto, *Thomas Jefferson and the American Ideal* (1987)

INDEX

About the Contributors

William L. Beiswanger

Robert H. Smith Director of Restoration at Monticello, Mr. Beiswanger has overseen numerous landscape and building restoration projects at Monticello. He is a contributor to the National Trust books *American Landscape Architecture* and *Master Builders,* and the author of *Monticello in Measured Drawings.*

Susan R. Stein

Curator of Monticello since 1986, Ms. Stein has responsibility for Thomas Jefferson's world-famous house and the wide variety of artifacts that relate to Jefferson's life on the mountain. She organized the landmark 1993 exhibition that commemorated the 250th anniversary of Jefferson's birth and produced the exhibition catalog *The Worlds of Thomas Jefferson at Monticello.*

Peter J. Hatch

Director of Gardens and Grounds since 1977, Mr. Hatch is responsible for the care, restoration, and interpretation of Jefferson's Monticello landscape. He is an authority on Jefferson's gardening interests and on the history of plants in American gardens. His most recent book is *The Fruits and Fruit Trees of Monticello.*

Lucia C. Stanton

Formerly Director of Research, Ms. Stanton is Shannon Senior Research Historian at Monticello. The author or co-editor of various books on Jefferson, including *Jefferson's Memorandum Books, Free Some Day: The African-American Families of Monticello,* and *Slavery at Monticello,* she is currently involved in an oral history of the descendants of Jefferson's slaves, which is part of her research on the African-American families of Monticello and on the plantation at large.

(Left to right) Lucia C. Stanton, William L. Beiswanger, Susan R. Stein, and Peter J. Hatch